"This book will break your heart and then put it back together again. It's an amazing testament to the way hope endures even in the midst of life's greatest tragedies."

— MARK BATTERSON
Lead pastor of National Community Church
in Washington, DC

"*Fear No Evil* tells the heart-wrenching tale of a church that was battered with tragedy but refused to be defeated, and a leader who perseveres knowing that the Lord has not left him. Brady Boyd is an example of absolute faith, one whose obedience and unfaltering focus on God's will cannot be shaken."

— PASTOR MATTHEW BARNETT
Founder of the Los Angeles Dream Center

"In *Fear No Evil*, we plunge with Brady and his congregation into the depths of the Valley of the Shadow of Death … literally! But, as promised, the gates of hell do not prevail, and from the heartache and brokenness, God brings healing, restoration, and … new life! This book is life changing!"

— WESS STAFFORD
President and CEO of Compassion International

"In *Fear No Evil*, Brady Boyd passionately tells the story of one of the worst possible nightmares, a church shooting. I found myself hurting, grieving, and crying with those who needlessly lost loved ones as Brady shared his firsthand account. But then he begins to unfold divine manna from heaven of God's plan to 'lead us through the valley of the shadow of death' with no fear. All of us have experienced tragedies and been attacked by fear. Brady is one of the best communicators I know, and *Fear No Evil* is definitely a book that will hold you riveted to the very end."

— PASTOR ROBERT MORRIS
Senior pastor of Gateway Church in Southlake, TX,
and bestselling author of *The Blessed Life*

"Brady Boyd is a vibrant, vital voice rising today — speaking with substance and solidity. His disarming simplicity brings a clarity and practicality that will encourage and refocus you."

— JACK W. HAYFORD
Founder and president of The King's University
in Los Angeles, CA

"Brady Boyd urges believers to cling to truth in a world that continues to give us trials. He exposes his own life journey with vulnerability in detail through hardships of church shootings and unexpected transitions. This book is an inspiration for believers to remain steadfast while running our life race with courage. We must fight for faith to hope and trust our heavenly Father, who gives the ultimate direction. In this marathon of life, *Fear No Evil* cries the message of truth to keep us running hard and looking to Jesus, the finisher of our faith."

— RON LUCE
President and founder of Teen Mania Ministries

"My personal observation of Pastor Brady Boyd in the moment of the shooting crisis at New Life confirmed to me the deep inward character I knew he had when he was recommended to be their senior pastor. I stood and watched as he looked down upon the bloodstains on the floor and walked out to face an army of media at the church entrance. He was calm, poised, compassionate, Spirit-led, and full of God's authority. His humble leadership not only settled a shaken church but also restored two broken families who had both lost children to the devil's devices. Read this book with a settled knowledge that God works in crisis and that the end result is that our lives, our characters, and our families will be stronger in the struggle."

— LARRY STOCKSTILL
Senior pastor of Bethany World Prayer Center
in Baton Rouge, LA, and overseer of New Life Church

"I have been close friends with Brady Boyd for over twenty years and serve as an overseer of New Life Church. I have personally witnessed the incredible courage and Christian character demonstrated by Pastor Brady and the congregation of New Life as they faced tribulation and tragedy with triumphant faith. This is a book that had to be written to tell a story that will inspire all who read it."

— JIMMY EVANS
Pastor of Trinity Fellowship Church and co-host of *Marriage Today*

"Few churches will ever be asked to endure tragedy at the level New Life Church experienced on December 9, 2007. But God is never caught off guard, and he put my friend Pastor Brady Boyd there for just such a time. Now Brady has written an incredible account of how God's amazing power can overcome tragedy and fear with forgiveness, worship, and joy."

— GREG SURRAT
Senior pastor of Seacoast Church, South Carolina

FEAR
NO EVIL

FOREWORD BY BILL HYBELS

FEAR
NO EVIL

A TEST OF FAITH, A COURAGEOUS CHURCH, AND AN UNFAILING GOD

BRADY BOYD
PASTOR, NEW LIFE CHURCH

ZONDERVAN.com/
AUTHORTRACKER
follow your favorite authors

ZONDERVAN

Fear No Evil
Copyright © 2011 by Brady Boyd

This title is also available as a Zondervan ebook. Visit www.zondervan.com/ebooks.

This title is also available in a Zondervan audio edition. Visit www.zondervan.fm.

Requests for information should be addressed to:
Zondervan, *Grand Rapids, Michigan* 49530

ISBN 978-0-310-32770-7

Published in association with the literary agency of Alive Communications, Inc., 7680 Goddard Street, Suite 200, Colorado Springs, CO 80920, www.alivecommunications.com.

Cover image: Getty Images®
Interior design: Beth Shagene

Printed in the United States of America

11 12 13 14 15 16 /DCI/ 24 23 22 21 20 19 18 17 16 15 14 13 12 11 10 9 8 7 6 5 4 3 2 1

To the tribe called New Life Church,
the most courageous and faithful people I have known.

Proceeds from *Fear No Evil* will go to the
New Life Church Dream Center in Colorado Springs,
a medical community outreach.

Contents

Ambassadors of Hope

WILLOW CREEK RECENTLY CELEBRATED ITS THIRTY-FIFTH ANNIVERSARY, and after the festivities had come and gone, during a quiet moment of reflection I thanked God for his goodness that has sustained us all these years. Like any church that has been around for a while, we have experienced ups and downs, good times and bad, seasons of blessing and those marked by immeasurable pain. By God's grace, we have prevailed.

Throughout those three-plus decades of ministry, I have seen too many churches wind up with a far different story to tell. Despite noble intentions and well-meaning commitments, adversity wins the day. The sequence is predictable and sad: calamity strikes and people scatter. They despise the sting, they fear the pain, they rush to disassociate from the mess. But not so with New Life Church. After suffering back-to-back blows that might have leveled another group, this courageous congregation chose to renew their faith, rally their energies, and doggedly rise again.

It is more than a feel-good story for New Life; it is good news for us all—because as churches reach for their redemptive potential instead of forfeiting the fight, increasing numbers of people wind up living lives that conform to the teaching Jesus offered and the example that he set. The net effect is a drastic reduction of the dangers of living on this planet. Think about this with me: if a few hundred million more people were to enter into a saving relationship with Jesus Christ over the next few years, and if they were then to start choosing inclusion over exclusion, righteousness over evil, serving over controlling, giving over grabbing, peace over violence, and love over hate, this world would be a far better place to live. This is why Jesus told us to pray each and every day that the will of his Father that is being played out to perfection in heaven would start to operate more and more here on planet Earth. Depravity may be on the loose today, but it doesn't have to be tomorrow. You and I can be agents of eternity-impacting change. We can be ambassadors—of compassion, of encouragement, of hope.

When pain hits home, most people's tendency is to want to run from it, replace it with another feeling, and pretend that they escaped unharmed. I experienced this most dramatically just after my dad died decades ago. The sadness that descended on me was so awkward and uncomfortable that I merely tried to pull myself together and move on. I returned to work and threw myself into a frenzy of ministry activity, counting on the chaos I was creating to distract me from the deep despair I felt.

But that is not God's way.

Instead, he encourages us to lean into the neediness we feel. He invites us to watch him bandage our wounds, set our broken bones, and start to stabilize things once more. He inspires us to slow down, review the loss, pray through it thoroughly, talk about it openly, think about it deeply, and write about it reflectively. Thankfully, that is exactly what Brady Boyd has done. And now, in these pages, you and I get to benefit from the lessons he learned along the way.

These days, whenever a round of suffering comes my way, the first thing I try to do—even before I allow myself the first taste of panic—is to try to grab hold of a foundational truth from God that I can cling to until things get sorted out. One that helps me every time is this: God is never, ever the author of evil. If I can't keep that particular truth straight in my mind, I am going to lose the plot every time. But if stay focused on the theological certainty that God *never* authors evil, then I stand a better-than-average chance of weathering the storm.

Throughout the Bible, God also promises that when we pass through the rising waters, we won't be walking alone. When we fight through the raging rivers, they will not sweep over us. When we walk through the furious fire, the flames will not set us ablaze. And when we trudge through life's darkest valleys, God promises he will always be there.

What's more, our good God limits the amount and the severity of the evil that comes our way so that it stays within our capacity to endure it. I don't know about you, but that kind of promise serves as a strategic part of my survival plan for life. Even when my circumstances unnerve me, I can hang onto that with my white-knuckled grip.

You may be reading this and thinking, "That's great for you, but you obviously don't understand how severe my suffering is." Deep down, you believe you are beyond hope, that life's rising waters are about to pull you under. But it's simply not the truth. The open tomb of Jesus Christ never stops tossing a life-preserver of hope to even the most hopeless of heart.

If you are going through a rough patch right now, I would ask you to consider by faith that just as God wove together something beautiful for the once-brokenhearted people known as New Life Church, he is at work behind the scenes in your life too. Despite how bleak and bitter and cold things may seem as you survey the landscape of your life, I promise you that God is working, just beyond what your eyes can see. He never sleeps, the Bible promises, and he never slumbers. He doesn't take the month off during your season of despair. On the contrary: Romans 8:28 says that for those who love God and follow him, he is working to make *all* wrong things right.

Take to heart the lessons from *Fear No Evil*. Don't wait for the next round of suffering to surface in your life before you confirm your belief that hope exists, that hope is available, and that hope will *always* prevail.

Bill Hybels
Founder and Senior Pastor
Willow Creek Community Church
South Barrington, Illinois

The Something God Asked Me to Say

MY FAMILY AND I LIVE ON THE PALMER DIVIDE, A RIDGE THAT SEPArates the basins of the Arkansas River and the Missouri River, and from our back deck the view is stunning. A long band of ponderosa pines stretches in front of five mesas that fill the distant landscape, and on most days when I'm hanging out back there, I'm joined by one form of Colorado wildlife or another.

Almost exactly two years after the shooting at New Life Church that took the lives of two of our congregation's young women, I was spending some private time with God on that deck, when he whispered a prompting to me. It wasn't an audible whisper, but the message was unquestionably clear. *I want you to write*, he said. *There is something I want you to say.*

The divine input caught me off guard. "Seriously?" I said out loud.

What has happened at New Life is miraculous, he continued. *It's a story I want you to tell.*

Immediately following the tragic events of December 9, 2007, I received a flood of offers to write a book. Politely I declined them all. First of all, I didn't feel it was my story to tell. Marie and David Works lost two daughters that day; if it was anyone's story, it was theirs. Moreover, I wasn't sure what I could offer readers going through the darker days of life, when I was still numb from my own pain.

But then God began to work on my heart, and on the hearts of the rest of our congregation. He bandaged our wounds, he shouldered our concerns, he shone a bright beam of light on what was at the time a very shadowy path. It took two long years for him to accomplish his work, but at last the broken places in our body were being made whole once again.

For several weeks following that prompting on the back deck, I mentioned the conversation between God and me to many of my trusted friends and mentors, and I asked what they made of the exchange. To a person, they agreed: "If God is asking you to write, then you need to write. This story needs to be told."

Still, I was less than convinced. My mind went back to a TV interview with famed football coach Lou Holtz, in which he said, "Most people talk until they say something...." I didn't want to be a guy who *wrote* until he said something. I'd read plenty of books whose authors seemed to fit that bill. And if what you're writing isn't revelation, then why bother publishing it in the first place?

But a miracle *had* occurred in our midst.

One of the interesting things about living at seventy-five hundred feet above sea level is that dense pockets of heavy fog can sock you in, even when everything is clear down below. On many foggy mornings as I make my way to work, I'll head down the hill toward the city of Colorado Springs and find a completely different world down there. Six minutes into my journey, the road is suddenly visible, the sky is bright, and the fog has disappeared.

That's how life feels at New Life Church these days. The fog has finally lifted. Our viewpoint has changed. Our perspective has shifted. Our outlook—at last—is bright. And ultimately, that's why I'm writing this book: if there is one message I hope to convey in these pages, it's that the bleak and devastating aftereffects of evil don't have to cloud your vision forever.

Our great God is committed to seeing you through.

Acknowledgments

THIS BOOK WAS TRULY A TEAM EFFORT. ALTHOUGH MY NAME IS ON THE cover, many others are equally responsible for it coming to fruition, first among them being my bride, Pam. She has been a solid rock of encouragement, prayer, and support throughout these past three years —and specifically over these many book-writing months. Her steadfast devotion to God and to me, and her transcendent peace, restore my soul each day.

My two kiddos, Abram and Callie, are simply the joy of my life. Their innocence and childlike faith make me see in fresh ways that God really will lead me through the darkest of valleys and celebrate with me atop life's highest mountains.

I am deeply thankful to the five men who serve not only as overseers for our fellowship but also as my close friends and confidants. Robert Morris, Tom Lane, Jimmy Evans, Jack Hayford, and Larry Stockstill were by my side during the most difficult days of December 2007 and have remained by my side ever since. Friends are a gift from God, and I am thankful to him for the wealth of wisdom each of these men has provided for New Life and for me.

I'm not sure how I would have navigated the uncharted seas of publishing without the wise guidance of Rick Christian, Joel Kneedler, and the team at Alive Communications. Glad I didn't have to find out.

Ashley Wiersma is a genius. That's a fact. She captured the heart and voice of this book and looked to the Holy Spirit for guidance at every turn as we crafted this story. Along the way, she became a mom for the first time and moved twice, and yet still found strength to put up with my sometimes-corny ideas.

I also appreciate the great team at Zondervan for believing in a first-time author and the power of this unique story.

Finally, I am so blessed to serve alongside the people of New Life Church, to whom this book is dedicated. Thanks for welcoming my family into your tribe of courageous and faithful people. We walked through the valley of the shadow of death, we conquered our fears, and somewhere along the way, we became a family.

PART 1

WHEN TRAGEDY STRIKES

That day, December 10, 2007, marked my hundredth day in my role at New Life. And in those hundred days, the original dreams I had for the church had been severely tested. What I couldn't know after three brief months was what God intended for us as a body. Would we forever be marked by the shameful or shocking behavior of others, or would we emerge with a different tale to tell? There was only one way to find out. And despite the evidence of a horror story having unfolded all around, I still found myself grateful to God that he had steered me New Life's way.

CHAPTER 1

The Day Nobody Hoped Would Dawn

We may not understand why a good God would allow
terrible suffering. But this merely establishes that if there
is a God, we do not know everything he knows.

Why should this surprise us?

— *Randy Alcorn*

CHRISTMASTIME HAD COME TO COLORADO SPRINGS. KIDS WERE GET-
ting out of school for holiday break, shopping centers were decked out
with ornamented trees and lights, carols flooded the radio airwaves,
and because of the spike in church attendance that always seems
to accompany Christmas and Easter, New Life was experiencing a
packed auditorium at every weekend worship service that month. Plus,
Pikes Peak had just been covered with a fresh blanket of snow, my wife
had dusted off her bison-chili recipe, and the NFL season was in full
swing. What wasn't to love about December 2007? It was my family's
first Christmas in Colorado, and all was going well.

In 2005, New Life debuted *Wonderland*, a theatrical production
put on by more than three hundred volunteers. In addition to ushering in the Christmas season, the performance also reaches out to
people from the community who don't know God, inviting them to

contemplate the message of Christ. It's a time to celebrate and rejoice and laugh, but also a time to worship the one true God.

On Friday and Saturday, December 7 and 8, 2007, New Life hosted thousands of people who had chosen to kick off the period known as Advent with this spectacular event: live performers ice-skating along a forty-foot catwalk, ballroom dancers twirling, animated fountains skipping, a drum line doing an incredible rendition of "The Little Drummer Boy," choirs lifting up all the familiar carols, actors in festive costumes portraying the traditional nativity scene — all culminating with a brief sermon and a candlelight closing.

My friend Dr. Jack Hayford was in town to speak at our Sunday morning services. I'd first met him when I was an elder and pastor at Gateway Church in Southlake, Texas, and for many years I had been impressed by his longevity in ministry — he began pastoring more than four decades ago — and by his great love for God and for God's people. Behind his back I referred to him as the apostle Jack. He has that sort of presence and power in a place, that of someone who has been sitting at the feet of Christ for many years.

Upon arriving at New Life as their new senior pastor, I discovered that Dr. Hayford had several connections to the church. He had served as a guest speaker on several occasions, he had dedicated the new sanctuary a few years prior, and the college that he founded and where he now serves as chancellor, King's College and Seminary, had an extension campus on New Life's property. But it had been a while since he had been back in Colorado Springs. I couldn't wait to give him a call, invite him to join us for a weekend soon, and reintroduce him to the people of New Life.

In addition to asking Dr. Hayford to come speak on the weekend of his choosing, once I had him on the phone I also inquired as to whether he would consider serving as one of our church's overseers — leaders from other churches and ministries who provide oversight and godly wisdom during both good times and bad. The role of overseer had become even more crucial recently because of the removal of New

Life's founding pastor. It told me a lot about Dr. Hayford's character when, despite his taxing obligations with King's College and Seminary and as president of the Foursquare movement that serves more than fifty thousand churches around the world, he responded with, "Whatever you need from me, you just let me know." He serves as a New Life overseer still today.

We decided that Dr. Hayford would fly in Saturday afternoon and then speak at both our nine o'clock and eleven o'clock services on Sunday morning, December 9. Afterward he and I would enjoy lunch together, and before he headed back to California, he would address a group of the King's Seminary students who meet at New Life, in order to provide some encouragement for overcoming the various challenges seminarians face.

On Saturday night I would deliver the brief closing sermon at *Wonderland*, and knowing how much Dr. Hayford loves music and performing arts — often as he heads down Interstate 405 in Los Angeles traffic, he has been known to "air conduct" whatever orchestral arrangement is on the radio with whichever hand is not on the wheel — I invited him to join me. He enthusiastically accepted even before I finished giving the rationale for why I thought he would enjoy it.

As expected, we both loved the performance, and as we were leaving the building to head to our respective cars in the parking lot, we bumped into the three wise men, still in full costume from the show. We all had our photo snapped together, and then I wished Dr. Hayford a good night's rest. I knew he was anxious to get to bed so he would be fresh for the next morning's activities. It had been a great evening, and as I drove to my house a few miles from the church, I had the distinct sense that we were in for a wonderful Sunday.

What was already a joyous season felt even sweeter, because we had begun to turn a corner. The church had suffered a major blow with the scandalous departure of Pastor Ted Haggard thirteen months prior because of moral misconduct, but now we could finally move on. Christmas is a time of birth and new life, and we as a body were ready for something great to be born. Certainly, there still were issues to tend to. But it felt as though we were all inhaling fresh air for the first time in almost a year.

Having a guest speaker take the pulpit on Sunday morning is like being handed a vacation day. I get to serve as host and hang out with the teacher who graciously has agreed to let me off the hook for a few hours. Talk about relaxing! Don't get me wrong; I love my job. But I also enjoy a break every now and then. If all went according to plan, I would enjoy Dr. Hayford's message (twice), I would pelt him with my latest laundry list of ministry-related questions over lunch in my office, I'd see him off to the Colorado Springs airport, and then I'd head home to watch my eleven-and-one Dallas Cowboys demolish the Lions while my family and I relished a snowy, lazy afternoon.

But all would not go according to plan.

The morning of December 9 began routinely enough: I woke before my wife, Pam, or our kids, Abram and Callie, had gotten out of bed. I showered and dressed and then headed to the church offices around 7:00 a.m. After pouring a cup of hot coffee, I sat down to spend a few moments of solitude with God and ask him for wisdom for the day. Eventually my thoughts drifted to the introductory comments I would need to make for Dr. Hayford before he took the stage at each service. As I jotted down a few things I didn't want to forget to mention to the congregation, I heard a rapid knock on my office's heavy wooden door.

Opening the door, I found the head of our church's volunteer security team standing in the hallway. He wondered if I had heard about the deadly shootings that had taken place the previous night in Arvada, Colorado, a town about sixty-five miles north of New Life. Evidently, just after midnight two young adults — Tiffany Johnson, aged twenty-six, and Philip Crouse, twenty-four — were shot and killed at a missionary training center for Youth with a Mission (YWAM) by a man who reportedly had been asking for a place to stay for the night. When the man was refused entry, he opened fire.

I intentionally avoid all media on Sunday mornings so I can stay focused on our gatherings as a church. The news came as a total shock to me.

"I think we should beef up security, just in case," the security officer said, to which I responded, "Good idea."

I didn't blink at consenting to the extra security presence; this is just the reality we live in today. If you're my age or older, you likely grew up in a setting where churches weren't preoccupied with protecting against gunmen who might burst into a church building ready to kill. But these days? It's a very real concern.

One Wednesday night in September 1999 — the same year that the Columbine High School tragedy erupted in Littleton, Colorado — a man walked into a worship service at Wedgwood Baptist Church in southwestern Fort Worth, Texas, and began shooting at the congregation. Seven people would lose their lives and seven more would be hospitalized — some with life-threatening injuries — before the gunman would turn his nine-millimeter on himself.

In March 2005, the eighty-member congregation of Living Church of God gathered at the local Sheraton Hotel in Brookfield, Wisconsin, their regular meeting space, for what was to be an ordinary Saturday evening worship service. Moments later one of their own congregants — a forty-four-year-old man said to have been suffering from depression — opened fire with an automatic weapon and killed the pastor, the pastor's son, and five other church members. Four other church members were wounded before the shooter took his own life.

Fourteen months later, in May 2006, an estranged husband and father named Anthony Bell stepped inside the Ministry of Jesus Christ Church, which met in an old warehouse in Baton Rouge, Louisiana, shot four people dead, kidnapped his wife and three children, and fled. An hour and a half later another shooting was reported at a nearby apartment complex. When police arrived on the scene, they discovered that Bell had shot and killed his wife in her own home.

Because of an ugly history when it comes to church shootings—not to mention the YWAM shootings the night before—I knew we couldn't be too careful. The security guard excused himself, I presumed so that he could go call in volunteer reinforcements for the morning's services, and I went back to preparing my remarks.

As I consider the day in hindsight, throughout that entire morning I never gave the Arvada shootings another thought. I had a couple of sidebar conversations with a few of the key pastors during and between worship services, but that's about it. I didn't know the people who had been killed at that YWAM center, and while I felt awful that innocent people's lives were taken from them in such a senseless act of violence, it wasn't an event that had any context for me. I liken it to when you come upon a terrible car accident on the other side of the freeway as you're cruising along at seventy miles an hour. For a split second, you feel the sting of sadness over what obviously just happened, but within a nanosecond your thoughts are trained once more on getting wherever it is you are going. Plus, the security team at New Life is as sharp as they come. Why fret about the hypotheticals, when our folks were already unflinchingly prepared?

When Ted Haggard was leading the church, his national status as president of the National Association of Evangelicals warranted extra precaution in and around the campus. At the time, the security team was all volunteer, but the men and women who served—some of whom were ex-military and many of whom were ex-law enforcement—were well-trained officers who took seriously their role of protecting the entire church from anyone who might be interested in disrupting a Sunday morning.

In addition to Ted's prominence, New Life was and is a very big congregation. At its height, attendance crested fourteen thousand worshipers every Sunday morning, which is roughly equal to the population of places such as Galena, Illinois, or Siloam Springs, Arkansas.

When you're dealing with a small town's worth of people week in and week out, situations always crop up. A toddler gets a scrape on his knee running around in the nursery. A kid falls off a piece of playground equipment and breaks an arm. An elderly woman slips and fractures a hip. An ailing man suffers a heart attack between stanzas 1 and 2 of "Awesome God." There is *always* something going on that requires immediate attention, and our security team was fully equipped to manage such circumstances.

But they also had done drills to prepare for more serious events. They had plans in place in case a fire broke out, a tornado struck, or —heaven forbid—a gunman set foot on the campus. They trained regularly on defensive tactics, they shot together at local practice ranges, and they talked openly about what they would do if an armed person ever threatened the well-being of New Lifers. "Part of our strategy," one of the team members later explained, "was that in the face of an active shooter, we all would assemble in a diamond formation, and whoever was in uniform would take the lead. We then would move swiftly through the building, focused solely on taking out the gunman, in order to prevent any further damages."

They also determined that in such a scenario, once Colorado Springs police officers arrived on the scene, all New Life security team members were to comply fully with official orders. Despite their solid training and in some cases vast experience, they knew to defer to our city's formally sanctioned personnel.

So, as I say, this group knew their stuff. They had an entire list of contingencies to walk through in the event that the worst unfolded at New Life. I just don't believe that anyone on that team thought they'd actually be asked to walk through those plans anytime soon.

The crowds on Sunday morning were thinner than usual. It had snowed the night before, and while we certainly weren't experiencing blizzard conditions, it was cold and messy enough outside to cause some people to choose their down comforters over the warmth of Christian fellowship.

Dr. Hayford delivered a powerful sermon during both services, and afterward four of us—Dr. Hayford and his assistant, Bill, as well as Pastor Ross Parsley and me—sat down at a small table in my office to eat lunch. We barely had blessed our meal when my assistant, Karla, rapped on the door, rushed into the room before I had time to answer her knock, and said, "Pastor Brady, there is gunfire in the building."

Karla Leathers is a steady woman; for me to hear alarm in her voice and see a flash of terror in her eyes meant that something was urgently wrong. What's more, as soon as she'd opened the door, all of us inside could hear the rapid *pop, pop, pop* of gunfire a floor below.

Like most boys raised in the wetland parishes of northwest Louisiana, I became a hunter shortly after I learned to walk, and therefore I know my way around guns. Handguns, shotguns, rifles—you name it, and I can tell you what it looks like and what it sounds like. My office at New Life is on the second floor, just over the main corridor of the children's wing, and when Karla had flung open the door, I knew that the bursts cracking the air were those of automatic gunfire.

I didn't have a lot of fright-filled moments on December 9, but one I did experience occurred immediately as I took in those sounds. My wife, Pam, is typically one of the last people to leave the building on Sunday mornings. She attends the late service and afterward seems to always get pulled into long conversations, which she loves to be part of. But what it means is that when everyone else has already left the campus, driven away, and sat down at a local restaurant, Pam is still meandering around the halls of New Life Church. The single question that crossed my mind was, "Is my family in that hallway right now?"

Rushing to my desk to retrieve my cell phone, I was having trouble regulating my breathing. I punched the speed-dial key that would connect me to Pam's phone, and when I heard her say, "Hello?" I felt my lungs exhale at last.

"Honey, where are you?" I asked as my heart settled into a steadier rhythm. In a drive-through lane, she replied. She had pulled away from the campus five minutes earlier and was getting the kids something to eat. The information relaxed me. Air filled my lungs, clarity returned to my mind, and all was well once more. Except that it was not.

"Pam, listen," I said. "Please do *not* come back to the church, but I need you to know that there have been shots fired on the campus. Please go straight home. I'm going to send someone to stay with you until I can get there."

What I didn't know at the time was that for some reason that Sunday, our children's pastor, Jeff Drott, a dear family friend who had also served at Gateway when Pam and I were there, decided he would save Pam a few steps after the eleven o'clock service was over. Instead of her having to come all the way down the children's hallway to retrieve our children, Pastor Jeff walked Abram and Callie to the sanctuary to find their mom. As a result, Pam never was in the children's ministry wing on the afternoon of December 9. Our friend had never walked our kids to the sanctuary before that day, and he hasn't done it since. It was a onetime prompting from God to Jeff that I believe protected my family.

Back in my office, as gunfire continued down below, it was Pastor Jeff whom I called next. After ensuring that he and his family were safe, I asked him to head over to my house and stay there until I could get home. When I ended that call, I began dialing as many pastors and leaders as I could think of, desperately seeking information on everyone's whereabouts and safety. My immediate instinct was to race downstairs to the children's wing to make sure that our congregation's kids all were okay, but I knew that the security guard who had been positioned outside my office during my lunch with Dr. Hayford wouldn't have allowed that. But what else was I supposed to do? Stay put while members of our congregation were running for their lives?

As it turned out, that's exactly what I did. That's what all of us who were gathered in my office did. And it was agonizing. From my second-story window, we watched helplessly as men, women, and children flew out the main doors, their arms shielding their heads from the threat of gunfire in the air, and raced to their cars as fast as their legs could take them. I had never before seen such a heart-wrenching scene and suspect I never will.

It wasn't until much later that I learned the horrors of what was unfolding all around me. According to police reports, around 1:00 p.m. on Sunday, December 9, a twenty-four-year-old man named Matthew Murray drove onto our campus with intent to kill. I don't know if he had been to our church before, but his actions lead me to believe he knew our systems quite well. He seemed to know that we have two layers of security, for instance — a layer of uniformed officers who help with traffic flow on Sunday mornings, and a layer of volunteer guards, some of whom are armed, whose job it is to protect the inside of the buildings during large events, including weekend worship services.

As Matthew Murray pulled in that day, he caught sight of a marked police car that was still patrolling our campus. According to eyewitnesses, he retreated and evidently waited for the cop to depart before beginning his mission of death and destruction, one that began with a diversion tactic. After he surmised that the final uniformed officer had left the premises, Murray drove to the west side of the main building and tossed out a military-grade smoke bomb. He then wheeled back around to the building's east side, where he parked his car.

Reports from various passersby later interviewed by local detectives indicate that Matthew Murray removed his keys from the ignition, laid his head on his steering wheel, and began to mumble something. As soon as he emerged from his vehicle, the shooting began. First he fired on a white minivan from twenty or thirty yards away, a van belonging to David and Marie Works, members of our congregation who commuted from Denver to be part of our fellowship each weekend. The entire Works family — the parents and their four daughters, Laurie,

Stephanie, Rachel, and Grace — were loading into their vehicle to head to a nearby restaurant for lunch. But that lunch would never take place. Moments after Matthew Murray began firing his weapon, eighteen-year-old Stephanie Works would lose her life, sixteen-year-old Rachel Works would be forced to fight in vain for hers, and David Works would be debilitated by a series of shots to his abdomen.

From there, the gunman shot at an SUV owned by New Lifers Judy and Matt Purcell. They and their three daughters were leaving the parking lot when Judy, who was sitting in the front passenger seat, suffered injuries to her shoulder and face. Matt sped off to the hospital, as Matthew Murray continued his rampage. He entered New Life's main building through the bank of glass doors that leads to the children's ministry wing. In his backpack and strapped to his chest were more than one thousand rounds of ammunition, two pistols, and an AR-15 semiautomatic assault rifle. There were still hundreds of people milling about at one o'clock that day, and Murray's ammunition supply and the big banana clip he boasted indicated he had plans to take down all of them.

But what Matthew Murray did not know was that our security team had not bought his initial smoke bomb ploy. Credit it to God's divine intervention or to the energetic and sometimes rambunctious kids hanging around New Life on any given day — either way, our guards are savvy when it comes to pranks. When the head of our security team that day, stationed at a central location inside the building, got word of the grenade, he deployed two guards to go check it out and asked a third guard to stay put.

As soon as shots could be heard from the children's wing, that lone security guard raced toward the commotion. After establishing a tactical position in an adjacent hallway, she stepped out to discover that Matthew Murray was shooting from more than sixty feet away. Pacing toward Murray, she fired her nine-millimeter ten times in an attempt to stop his rage-filled efforts. Four of those shots connected, and after the fourth, he crawled into another hallway, where he would inhale his last breath.

Real time, I had no idea what was going on. For forty-five minutes following my assistant's initial report that there were shots being fired in the building, and at the explicit instruction of our security team, Dr. Hayford and the others and I were under lockdown in my office. "When I leave this office," one security guard had said, "I want you to close this door, lock it, and do not allow entry to anyone but my team or the SWAT team." Police were on their way, he assured us, and as soon as he had more information, he would be back.

After following his instructions to a tee, I headed toward the windows to pick up any clues I could find. Within three minutes the parking lot was a crush of police cars, ambulances, fire engines, and drug enforcement agency vehicles, with helicopters hovering overhead. Lights were flashing, sirens wailed, and my cell phone kept lighting up. With each call, I received one more puzzle piece that shaped a picture I did not want to see. But then came the report that perhaps things weren't as bad as they seemed. "Brady," one guard said over the phone, "we have two minor injuries, one arm and one shoulder. But the gunman has been subdued. I'll update you when I can."

In that moment, I thought, "Wow. What an unbelievable miracle of God." To have a person bent on violence open fire on your church campus and have its members suffer only two minor injuries as a result —I was relieved at a level I found difficult to put into words. In fact, those of us in my office had been praying fervently for everyone's protection, and as that new information washed over me, I asked the group to stop once more and pray prayers of gratitude to God. But our prayer was interrupted by news of another kind.

"Brady, we're getting word that there may be a second shooter," came the update. Evidently, some activity had been spotted atop the World Prayer Center, a one-story facility with a high-pitched roof that is positioned just outside our main building, within line of sight of my office windows. "You and your guests need to stay put in your office,"

I was told, "but get as far away from the windows as you possibly can. We fear a sniper may be involved."

Thankfully, it turned out to be a false report. I'm still not sure who saw what on the roof of the prayer center, but Matthew Murray acted alone that day.

Additional reports would follow that one, some erroneous and some accurate. My colleagues and I were desperate for information, but the burden of sorting out truth from fiction was more than a little tough to bear.

Nearly an hour after Karla's entrance into my office, there was a heavy pounding on the door. "SWAT team," a voice called out. "Please open up." Not considering that even *that* could have been a ploy, I stepped quickly to the door, unlocked it, and eased it open. We were promptly told that various SWAT units were conducting a sweep of the entire three-hundred-thousand-square-foot facility, walking room by room throughout the campus, and ushering anyone who was found away from the main building and across the street to the Tent, a smaller, bubble-shaped building that we use for various worship services and activities during the week.

We were asked to follow the armed guard who would escort us to the Tent, where each person's statement would be taken by uniformed Colorado Springs officers. The process of getting to that secondary location will go down as one of the strangest memories I carry from that admittedly *very* strange day. Not only were we asked to follow the guard in single-file formation, but we were also made to stick our hands in the air in something of an "I surrender" posture, just in case one of us was somehow involved in the incidents that had unfolded. I was walking just behind Dr. Hayford, and as I watched him follow in lockstep behind the officer, his hands thrust high into the sky as though he were a common criminal, I thought, "I wonder if he'll ever come speak here again."

Sometimes funny things like that cross your mind during life's most intense moments, which I think may be further evidence of

God's goodness and grace. Having something else to focus on—even momentarily—was just the dose of relief I needed.

As we entered the Tent, I noticed three hundred or so people already gathered there, all of whom had been somewhere on campus when the gunfire erupted. Police officers asked each of us if we had seen the shooter, if we knew the shooter, if anyone had heard him say anything, and so forth. The process of documenting all three hundred statements took several hours, but the information those interviews yielded would prove vital to the integrity of the investigation.

Within moments of entering the Tent, I caught sight of a woman sitting in the middle of the room, her head down, her face in a state of shock, her shirtfront covered in blood. Her hands were bloodstained too, and as I took in her body's panicky shakes, I realized I had not been told everything.

I walked up to her and said, "Ma'am, what happened?" But she could not respond. A young woman and a girl, whom I presumed to be her daughters, were seated by her side. Appearing equally distraught, the older one said in a weak voice, "Two of my sisters were shot. My dad was also shot. And the ambulances took them away."

Looking into the mother's eyes, I saw fright and distance there. Although I didn't know it yet, I was face-to-face with Marie Works, mother of Stephanie and Rachel Works, the two girls who would not live to see another day dawn.

Immediately I gathered everyone who was inside the Tent into a massive huddle that surrounded Marie and the eldest and youngest of her four daughters, Laurie and Grace. "Friends," I announced, "this family is really suffering right now, and I'd like for us to stop what we're doing and pray for them all." Reflexively, New Lifers pressed into the center of the room, those closest to the women and young Grace placing their outstretched hands on their shoulders, their arms, their knees. We prayed by faith that God would intervene in that family's suffering, that he would protect Stephanie, Rachel, and David, all of whom were at a local hospital by then. We prayed that he would guide surgeons' hands and that he would sustain his children with his unfailing promise of provision. We prayed soul-level prayers, prayers of those who have just endured a terrible ordeal together. And when we opened our eyes once more, that room was flooded with a certain peace that I'll remember for a long, long time. God saw us, he cared for us, and he still held us all in his grip. I was certain of those things, despite uncertainty on every other front.

As the tight jumble of people disbanded, I sat down beside Marie and talked with her for a few more minutes. I could tell from her comments that she and her family were very well connected at New Life and that they had a support system that was quite strong. From all sides of the room, she had people tending to her; knowing she was in good hands, I stood and eased away.

As I did, a medical doctor who is a member of our church, Brian Olivier, approached me and said quietly, "Brady, I need to talk to you."

He pulled me aside, away from the larger group, and said, "Listen, I was there in the parking lot when everything erupted. I tried to give care to the two girls and their dad after they had been shot.

"The girls are not going to live," he continued. "In fact, the older of the two died instantly. She took a shot — probably into the aorta — and was gone within a minute or two of impact. Her sixteen-year-old sister, Rachel, took several shots in the thorax and I imagine has died en route to the hospital. The dad had several wounds in his abdomen, but I suspect he will survive."

As Dr. Olivier talked, my mind raced and my heart seemed to detach itself from the rest of my body. I'm a pastor. Pastors pastor people. They show compassion and care and love to people. They tend to people's needs, but given the size of the needs we now so clearly faced, I thought I might utterly come undone. "What happened here today?" I thought. "What *really* happened?"

James 1:5 says, "If any of you lacks wisdom, he should ask God, who gives generously to all without finding fault, and it will be given to him." In that moment of real despair, I could think only to beg God for wisdom, to ask him for clarity regarding the next steps I should take. "Father, I need you," I whispered. "I need your wisdom, and I need your strength. I need insight that only you can provide."

Just then Dr. Hayford approached me, which felt about as close to an in-person visit from God as you can get. He is tall and has a towering and stately presence about him, combined with integrity that is obvious to all. Placing his heavy hands on my shoulders and looking me squarely in the eyes, he said, "Brady, forty years ago when I was a young pastor, we had something tragic happen at our church too. God provided me an extra measure of grace in order to make really good decisions during that time. Brady, God's grace is going to be with you now, and you are not going to make a bad decision for ten days' time. For the next ten days, you are going to make *only* good decisions."

My response to Dr. Hayford's prophetic declaration was a mixed bag. Sure, I was encouraged by the prospect of manifesting wise leadership. But ten days? As long as we were prophesying, why not shoot for a month or even a year?

I kept to myself my request for an extension and simply received the words that had been spoken. What neither Dr. Hayford nor I knew at the time was that it would be exactly ten days from the day of the shooting until the day when we as a church would lay Stephanie and Rachel Works to rest. Their dad would be recovering in a hospital bed all that time and wouldn't be strong enough to attend a funeral until precisely ten days had passed. It was a time frame that represented closure somehow, and until that sense of closure occurred, God protected me from making mistakes. Of course I led imperfectly, but in terms of feeling equipped to manage the bigger dilemmas I would face over that coming week and a half, I sensed God's presence in a powerful way. There is no handbook for pastors on how to deal with a heavily armed gunman roaring through your church, but because of Dr. Hayford's profound words, I was reminded that God is still God, even when the stakes are unbelievably high. I had not been forsaken or left to my own leadership whims. I had the God of all creation by my side, willing to direct every step I needed to take.

Two and a half hours after SWAT team members led me from my office to the Tent, I was asked to give a press conference so the congregation and the community at large would hear directly from me the details of what had happened on our campus that day.

The group of us who had been assembled by police officers were finally released, and soon thereafter I alerted our church's attorney that I was ready to address the media pool that had gathered near the main building's north entrance. Stepping outside, I realized I had neglected to grab an overcoat that morning, and quickly I was shivering from the chill in the air. Despite the turquoise-blue skies above, it was December in Colorado. And I was cold. Our attorney removed his heavy black coat, thrust it over my shoulders, and stayed right by my side as I stepped up to the bouquet of microphones that seemed to form out of nowhere.

I had no idea what I was going to say — or what I was *supposed* to say during such a time. I have a journalism background, so I suppose somewhere in the recesses of my mind I knew instinctively the type of questions I would be asked: Where was I when the shooter entered the building? Did I have a description of the gunman? Did I know the shooter? Did I know any possible motive for why the shooter would want to harm people at New Life? Was this the same shooter who killed two in Arvada the previous night?

But none of those details mattered much to me then. What I was focused on was the families of those who had been injured or killed, and the congregation at large, many of whom had witnessed truly terrible things that day, things that stand in stark contrast to what we think of when we think of church.

Trusting God to place words on my tongue, I began to speak.

"What happened today was a real tragedy," I said. "People lost their lives today. They came to church to worship. They came to church with their families to *worship*, and what happened today was a real tragedy."

I told those reporters and anyone who happened to be watching the news feed that as a pastor, I felt as if my heart was absolutely broken. I acknowledged how unfortunate it is that we live in a society where things like that happen, and I assured everyone within the sound of my voice that despite the difficult day it had been, New Life Church would in fact prevail.

After thanking the many first responders who acted so valiantly on New Life's behalf, I called on the entire city of Colorado Springs to pray for the families of those who had been harmed during the shooting. I gave out information on where New Lifers who had witnessed various aspects of the horrifying sequence of events could find immediate help by way of crisis counseling. And I thanked Colorado Springs for being the kind of city that rallies around those who are hurting, a city that looks after each other the way that we do. I had been a resident there for a whopping four months. But already it was clear to me that it was a community that genuinely cares.

There would be a second news conference nearly three hours after the first; unfortunately, I didn't have many more details to share. I confirmed that the Works girls and their father had been shot and asked for prayer on behalf of all the families of those who had been injured or traumatized. And then, finally, I was allowed to leave the campus for the day. Actually, local police officers insisted on it; they had an investigation to conduct and needed the buildings and surrounding parking lots completely cleared in order to finish it.

It was close to seven in the evening when I arrived at Penrose Hospital, a facility just north of downtown Colorado Springs that is known for its stellar trauma-unit care. My primary goal was to connect with the Works family. By that time, Stephanie had been pronounced dead, and Rachel remained on life support. David was still in surgery, but I was able to talk and pray with many of his family members and friends.

The scene at Penrose was heartrending. I couldn't help but notice all of the New Lifers and other residents of Colorado Springs who were already there, praying, caring, serving those who had been most significantly impacted during the shooting. Meals and flowers were already arriving, transportation needs were being sorted out, and someone had even volunteered to go purchase a change of clothes for Marie, Laurie, and Grace Works, since their church clothes had been bloodied in the shooting and their home was an hour's drive away.

After talking with doctors, nurses, and others who were tending to members of our church who had been wounded in various sprays of gunfire, I offered to pray with as many people as I could, asking God for comfort, for healing, for the eradication of fear, for confidence in his ability to work *all* things together for good. And then I headed home. After all, I had a wife and two beautiful kids whom I hadn't seen all day. I was long overdue for some hugs, for a break from the rigors of the day.

Around nine thirty, I pulled into the garage of our home in northern Colorado Springs and exhaled the weight I had been carrying since just after one o'clock that afternoon. It occurred to me that I hadn't had time or space to let my emotions catch up to all I had experienced, but no sooner had the thought crossed my mind than Pam came out from the house to the garage. She must have heard me pull in, and at the sight of her — my gorgeous, faithful, perfectly *safe* wife — I came undone. As tears flowed, we were silent. But in our silence we were thinking the same thing. We were so grateful that no one in our family had been hurt, and at the same time we were devastated that the Workses had lost two daughters. We were grieving the other injuries and the loss of innocence for our church. So many emotions, wrapped up in soundless tears.

Several minutes passed in that garage — ten, maybe — before both of us realized we'd be much warmer inside. We headed into the house, where I saw Pastor Jeff and his wife, Jenny. Faithful to the core, they had stayed at Pam's side all day long. What a gift to have friends like that.

The ten of us—Jeff and Jenny and their four kids, Pam, our kids, and me—gathered in the living room, where I conveyed the most recent information I had been given from New Life security, New Life staff members, hospital personnel, family members of people hurt in the shooting, and so forth. The more I talked, the more drained I became. The day was finally wearing on me, from the inside out.

To neither Pam's nor my surprise, Abram and Callie understood exactly what had unfolded at their church that afternoon. Even at ages nine and seven, they grasped that someone had come to our campus to do very bad things, and that another person had been forced to stop him before the bad guy could hurt more people than he already had. Callie asked, "Dad, did he come on the campus to shoot you?"

Feeling too weary to do anything but tell the plain truth, I said, "Callie, he came on the campus to shoot all of us. We all were victims today."

Satisfied with the facts, as kids so often are, she and her brother hugged me tightly and then headed off to bed. In their little world, as long as Dad was home, safe and sound, all was well once more. Plus, they had been spared the gruesome sights and sounds of the tragedy and had no awful memories needing to be worked through. They had been miles away from the church by the time destruction rained down. For that I'll always be grateful.

Sitting in my living room that night, as Jeff and Jenny absorbed everything I said, there were questions and then tears, more questions and then more tears. Finally it was time for someone to get some sleep. All of our bedtimes had come and gone, and I knew they probably missed their own home. I thanked them profusely for dropping everything and loving my family well that day, and then Pam and I wished them all a good night.

As they were leaving, my cell phone rang. It was one of our pastors,

Rob Brendle, with news that Rachel Works indeed had passed away. The information was a devastating end to a truly tragic day.

Although sleep was what I craved more than anything else that night, I found it incredibly difficult to calm my mind, to relax my tense muscles, to tend to my unsettled soul. Staring at the shadows that were casting odd shapes across the ceiling, I considered the invitation that Dr. Hayford had extended to our congregation during his sermon that morning. Was it really just this morning that he spoke? How could one single day take a lifetime to elapse?

Addressing the well-known story in Matthew 2 of the magi coming to the Christ child upon his birth and offering up their gifts, Dr. Hayford had said, "May we all be like the wise men, who not only came with exaltation for the King, but also came with expectation for an *encounter* with him. Scholars can know the Scriptures without ever knowing the Savior. May we never settle for knowing *about* this Christ. May we insist on *encountering* him as well."

Before he closed the service, Dr. Hayford explained that one of his hopes this Christmas was to have a heart that was soft before the Lord. "Softheartedness is not softheadedness," he clarified. "Having a soft heart toward the Lord means having a heart that is shapeable, a heart that is imminently correctible, a heart that can be taught and imprinted, a heart that is understanding toward others, a heart that is patient. And a heart that is *forgiving.*"

How desperately those of us who called New Life our home, myself included, would need to manifest that last characteristic — not weeks or months or years later but beginning right there and then.

CHAPTER 2

Departures and Arrivals

What seems a hindrance becomes a way.
— Henri Nouwen

IF I DID SLEEP THE NIGHT OF THE SHOOTING, IT WAS FITFUL SLEEP AT best. Monday morning brought with it the all-over ache that comes with having pulled an all-nighter, even though I had been in bed for seven hours straight. I dressed quickly, knowing that the demands of the day weren't waiting for me to feel energized or awake. Representatives from the Colorado Springs police department would be arriving at the main entrance of the church in order to allow a few senior staff members to view the crime scene, and I didn't want to keep them waiting.

Along with several of New Life's pastors — Garvin McCarrell, Rob Brendle, Ross Parsley, Lance Coles, Brian Newberg — I stepped inside the church building and found a war zone at my feet. A church's building normally is a place of comfort and joy and peace, but all I saw before me was blood and bullet holes. Something had to be done, and fast. Neither my colleagues nor I wanted our staff or congregation to be subjected to seeing New Life's facilities like that; disturbing images like those could take years to get over. Later that day, the church would be given the all-clear on the crime scene and allowed to return to the building. The next time our people came to the campus, we wanted them to experience order and a sense of peace.

A memory from that dreadful day-after I will carry with me for a long time involves Lance Coles, the longest-tenured pastor on our staff. When he and I and the other pastors entered the church building that morning, police officers had shown us the doors that had been shot to pieces, the hallways that were punctuated by ammunition shells, and the floor where the shooter had died. I swallowed hard as I stared at the large pool of dried blood that covered the space. By that time, we had already called for custodial help to come and clean the building. But that didn't matter to Lance.

Without saying a word, he tugged on rubber work gloves, reached for a scraper, crouched on his hands and knees, and laboriously sawed at the stain on the floor until that spot was shiny white. I stood there paralyzed by his presence of mind to tackle such a task, by his generosity of spirit, by how compelled he was to make right all that had gone so terribly wrong. As I watched him work, I thought, "How did we get here? How did I get here?"

Five months prior I had been enjoying a simple life in Dallas, Texas, working hard with ministry partners I admire, playing hard with a family I adore, relishing the warmth of summertime, living life to the full. But now? I was standing on the blood-soaked floor of the children's ministry wing in a church in Colorado Springs, the church where I was the senior pastor, the church where just yesterday a gunman had showed up and killed two of our congregation's girls.

The other pastors and I decided to shut down the building for several hours and spend the day returning it to its original beauty and cleanliness. A local glass company was called, and within the hour shot-out doors and windows were being replaced with fresh panes. Craftsmen showed up to swap out heavy doors that also had been riddled with bullets. Painters came to patch holes and roll a clean coat of white on the hallways that had been stained with blood. And ten or twelve folks from our church's hospitality team offered to work their magic on floors, carpets, and walls throughout the entire children's ministry wing. By four o'clock that afternoon, every inch of New Life Church was gleaming from ceiling to floor.

For my part, I tended to two more press conferences, where I spoke about the Works family's terrible losses and again offered the community information regarding counseling that was available for anyone affected by the shooting. There were many questions to answer — about how the girls died, about our affiliation (or lack thereof, as it turned out) with the shooter, about the undeniable heroism of New Life's security team. Afterward I headed back to Penrose Hospital to visit again with friends and family members of those who had been wounded. The scene was somber: David Works was still recovering from surgery and had just learned about his daughters' deaths. But despite his evident devastation, there was a remnant of hope in the air.

Predictably, it was turning out to be a draining day, but I knew I had to grind it out. On what seemed a too-frequent basis that Monday, I begged God for the strength to keep plugging along, knowing that at some point the frenetic pace I was maintaining surely would come to a halt. Or so I hoped, anyway.

By Wednesday night that week, my body would simply cave to the exhaustion I had been fighting. I can't remember another time in my life when I was so thoroughly wiped out as I was on that night. But today was Monday. My grand exhale would have to wait two more days.

If there was one saving grace on Monday, one source of energy, encouragement, and wisdom that helped me to stay the course, it was the presence of New Life's overseers, all of whom had dropped everything to stand by my side during a very dark week. Among them was Robert Morris, the founding and senior pastor of Gateway Church, and the man whom I fondly refer to as "my pastor." Those men formed something of a safety net for me, emotionally, spiritually, and practically. They were available for my questions. They were helpful as I made decisions, both large and small. They prayed over me and for me and were present the entire first part of that week. It's what the church does better than any other organism on planet Earth; it rallies around brothers and sisters during deeply troubling times and reminds the ones who are suffering that despite the darkness all around, the sun will once again shine.

That day, December 10, 2007, marked my hundredth day in my role at New Life. And in those hundred days, the original dreams I had for the church had been severely tested. What I couldn't know after three brief months was what God intended for us as a body. Would we forever be marked by the shameful or shocking behavior of others, or would we emerge with a different tale to tell? There was only one way to find out. And despite the evidence of a horror story having unfolded all around, I still found myself grateful to God that he had steered me New Life's way.

More than three years ago, during a day of fasting and praying, I sensed God saying to me, *Brady, you are about to turn onto a different path than the one you're on. There is a transition that is about to happen to you, and it involves your leaving Gateway Church.*

Thinking this was something of a dialogue, I said, "Well, where am I going, God?" but there was no real reply. Actually, I think I sensed him say something like, *Just follow me!* — which to a down-to-earth straight shooter like me is as good as silence.

But there was something to his counsel that stuck with me that day. Instead of acting like I had been brushed off by the King of the universe, I decided to take him at his word. If he was asking me to trust him and follow him and quit worrying about sorting out all the whens, wheres, and hows, then maybe that was exactly what I should do.

In John 16, Jesus offers some counsel to his disciples, all of whom are troubled that their fearless leader soon will be leaving them, at least in bodily form. Sensing their trepidation, Jesus tells them not to worry: he isn't going to leave them as orphans here on earth. In verses 12 and 13, he says, "I have much more to say to you, more than you can now bear. But when he, the Spirit of truth, comes, he will guide you into all truth. He will not speak on his own; he will speak only what he hears, and he will tell you what is yet to come."

"He will guide you into all truth." That promissory phrase hit me in fresh ways as I considered taking God at his word. It was as if he were committing to serve as my spiritual GPS, telling me just before each turn that it was time to go left, time to bear right, time to change lanes, and so forth. In essence, he said to me on that day of prayer and fasting, *If you will stay tuned to me, Brady, if you will listen to me, trust me, lean on me, and do exactly what I say to do, then I promise I will keep you on paths of righteousness. And if for some reason you choose to veer off, then I will recalculate and steer you back on course.*

God's commitment that day worked wonders on my questioning soul.

During my last few years as associate senior pastor at Gateway, I experienced several seasons of restlessness in my leadership role. Some people never feel that way; they are incredibly steady and never get the sense that they are supposed to be doing anything other than what they happen to be doing at that particular moment in life. I am not one of those guys.

Whenever that familiar restlessness crept in, I'd head for Senior Pastor Robert Morris's office and say, "I'm not sure if it's just boredom or what, but I think I need a new challenge."

The first few times I made the request, Robert would give me something else to do. He would hand me a new assignment, he would task me with something new to build, he would offer up a brand-new ministry for me to start, and I would be fired up each and every time. For a year or so following our exchange, I would get everything up and running, I would raise up new leaders, and I would fine-tune fresh systems. Then eventually I would find myself restless once more. Days later I'd be sitting in Robert's office again, singing the tune he now knew by heart. "Okay, so I don't know if it's just boredom or what," I'd say, "but I think I need a new challenge."

In January of 2007, I sat down with the other elders of Gateway and essentially told them I didn't think there was another challenge for me there. My words didn't shock them; Gateway has such a healthy environment that the elders and pastoral staff alike had invited me to speak candidly with them every step of the way. They knew that God was calling me to something new, and that very likely it would mean a departure from the church I loved.

We were at a five-day elders' retreat a few hours from the Dallas—Fort Worth metroplex, and during a frank discussion near the end of our time together, I explained to them what I had already told Robert privately, that the only other challenge I'd be interested in pursuing at Gateway was Robert's job. And since he was a good twenty- or twenty-five years from retirement, hanging around in hopes of becoming Gateway's next senior pastor simply wasn't an option. The six of them responded with customary graciousness. "Brady, we sense God's call on your life," they said. "Let us pray over you and for you, that you—and we—would have eyes to see and ears to hear what God is up to in your life."

An assistant snapped a picture of the group of us after that meaningful conversation, a photo that I have framed on my desk at New Life. Every time I catch sight of those men, I thank God for placing them in my path. Collectively and individually, they were treating my imminent departure from Gateway as a marriage, not a divorce. That's the view the Gateway elders chose to embrace.

I missed those men as I reflected on the transition to New Life Church. Without a doubt, it was their godly impact that helped me lead as well as I possibly could during the days after the shooting occurred.

* * *

Somewhere along the way, one of Gateway's elders encouraged me to send my resumé to New Life Church. He knew they were in search of a new senior pastor, and he knew I was still unclear about where my own transition was supposed to lead. At the time, I was in discussion with two churches, one in Florida and one in Arizona, about coming to serve as the lead person. In addition, I was considering planting a church in north Dallas. When the elder suggested the New Life role, I figured I didn't stand a chance. "I don't know a single person there," I said to him. "Plus, I'm not sure I would even *want* the role, given all the craziness that has gone on there."

Still, he encouraged me to try, which I did. I sent my resumé to New Life and, because of what happened next, believe it promptly got tossed in the trash. As part of their due diligence, the pastoral search committee at New Life wound up calling several trusted pastors from all over the nation, asking if they knew any godly leaders who might be a good fit at their church. One of the men they contacted was Jimmy Evans, pastor of Trinity Fellowship Church in Amarillo, Texas, and head of *Marriage Today* ministries. Jimmy himself wasn't interested, because he already was serving as senior pastor in a local church and enjoyed a thriving television ministry as well. But after conveying their preferences regarding the type of person who would fill New Life's role, the committee asked Jimmy for his input. He said, "Well, the best person for that job is someone whose resumé you've already seen."

"Who's that?" came the reply.

"Brady Boyd, from Gateway Church in Southlake, Texas."

They told Jimmy they had never seen my resumé but would definitely check to see what happened. Unable to find the paperwork I sent, they went online and listened to several talks I had given at Gateway. A few days later I received a call from Brian Newberg, who oversees New Life's administration function and was a member of the search committee.

The preliminaries behind us, Brian asked me, "Would you be at all interested in applying for the role of senior pastor?"

The ensuing conversation revealed to me that although the church had been embroiled in scandal for many months, the leaders who remained at New Life were committed to the integrity they'd always prized. I re-sent my information and then two weeks later learned that I had made the search committee's list of top-ten finalists. "Really?" I asked. I was stunned. Knowing I needed some time to try to sort out what God was up to with the New Life opportunity, I put all other pursuits on hold. I discontinued research on planting a church, and I suspended dialogue with the other two churches.

I would soon discover that the top ten would be narrowed to a top four, and that we four and our spouses would be flown to Colorado Springs for three days of in-person interviews with the entire search committee. In May of 2007, just four short months after my restlessness hit an all-time high, Pam and I boarded a jet at the Dallas–Fort Worth airport, bound for the Rocky Mountains. It would be a rigorous —and rousing—seventy-two hours, three days that would change life as we knew it forever.

The final day of Pam's and my visit to Colorado Springs brought with it bluebird skies and mild, springtime temps. I woke in our hotel room bed early that Friday morning and lay there awhile, considering all that the three days had held. By my estimation, the meetings had gone extremely well. I felt strangely encouraged about the opportunity, despite the initial qualms I'd had. Still, I craved some sort of divine validation, a word from God that would clarify whether the path I was supposed to follow happened to wind through Colorado Springs.

While Pam slept soundly, I gathered up my Bible and journal and headed into another room. From my seat on the couch, I had a postcard-perfect view of Pikes Peak through the west-facing window. It was stunning.

I was reading through the book of Nehemiah at the time, about all the frustrations and complications Nehemiah faced as he sought to rally a group of rather disgruntled people to rebuild Jerusalem's broken-down walls. It was inspiring to take in Nehemiah's courage, his persistence, his faith. Nothing seemed to get the guy down. God had given him a task to accomplish, and he was bound and determined to see it through.

As I reread the story that over the years I have come to know so well, I was reminded of another passage of Scripture, the verses in 1 Corinthians 3 that speak of the various roles God asks his people to play. Verses 6 and 7 say, "I planted the seed, Apollos watered it, but God made it grow. So neither he who plants nor he who waters is anything, but only God, who makes things grow."

I mulled over those verses and sensed God posing a series of questions to me. *Brady*, he asked, *do you think you could plant a church?*

In my spirit I told him that yes, I thought I could.

Then, *Brady, what if I called you to water something instead of plant it?* That question hung in the air for a few moments before God continued. *Specifically, what if I called you to New Life Church for the sole purpose of providing water to a body that was desperately in need of refreshment?*

Without a moment's hesitation I said, "I'll do either one, Lord." Some are called to plant, some are called to water, and I wanted to do whichever one God was calling me to do.

I glanced down at my open Bible and carried the thought further in my mind. Some are called to build something, and some are called to rebuild. Jerusalem had been an impressive city with strong and beautiful walls. But those walls had been torn down. And now someone was needed who would come along and do the often inglorious work of putting them back together again, brick by brick. Was this what God was asking me to do with New Life Church?

The Holy Spirit interrupted my thoughts. *Brady, if I called you to this assignment, would you take it?*

I hate to admit that even with all my ultraspiritual thinking that morning, now that the rubber was meeting the road, I slowed my speed quite a bit. After too long of a pause, I replied, "Lord, coming to New Life wouldn't exactly be a good career move. You know all that has gone on here. Whoever takes the reins next is in for quite a ride."

Certainly, there were far easier things to do. For all of the rigors involved in planting a church, even that would have been easier than coming here. Actually, any opportunity I could have chosen to pursue would have carried with it a boatload of challenges—planting a church, taking over a church in Florida or Arizona, and so forth. But *nothing* could have compared with the challenges of coming to Colorado Springs—and specifically coming to New Life Church. I sensed it then, and with the benefit of hindsight, I know it for sure now.

I asked one of my spiritual mentors one time about the dynamics involved in taking the lead role at an existing church. His counsel to me that day centered on three don'ts: don't ever follow the founding pastor, don't ever follow a senior pastor who either was very famous or had a thriving television ministry, and don't ever go to a church that is in the middle of a building campaign or has taken on extraordinary debt. Talk about having three strikes against me! If I took the New Life role, I'd be following the founding pastor, who was in fact famous, and heading into a leadership setting that was shadowed by many millions in debt.

In my most rational voice, there in the hotel room in Colorado Springs, with Pikes Peak standing majestically in the distance, I said, "God, surely you know that you're never to follow a founding pastor, you're never to follow a *famous* pastor, and you're never to walk headlong into a pile of massive debt."

God didn't seem overly concerned.

Figuring if ever there was a time to build my case, it was now, I then reminded God that the reputation of the church in question had been dramatically soiled. If you mentioned New Life Church in Colorado Springs to anyone in the country, you'd get a variety of strong reactions in response, and most would not be good. Plus, once momentum has come to a halt for a community of faith, it's immensely difficult to reenergize that church.

When you plant a church, part of the thrill is that you get to build it around a certain ethos. The young church grows and grows, becoming an unstoppable force for good in the world, and everyone is excited and energized by all that God is doing in their midst. But when you come to a church that is picking up post-scandal pieces, there is little energy to be found. It's sort of like the difference between driving a brand-new Ferrari off the showroom floor and opting to buy a banged-up beater that has been nearly totaled in a head-on collision. The desperate salesman's parting words are meant to counter the eyebrow you raised in suspicion: "It still functions, technically. It just needs some minor repairs if you plan to get anywhere fast."

From an occupational standpoint, I kind of wanted the souped-up sports car. I told God as much that day, and here is what I heard in reply: *Brady, I need someone to take this assignment who is not concerned first and foremost with his career.*

The insight led to a moment of real introspection for me. I was forced to reflect on my heart's posture and my deep-seated motivations. Was this transition just about taking the next step jobwise and moving up some sort of ladder, or was I truly interested in doing something important for the kingdom of God?

The role in question was going to be tougher than anything I had known, but I had learned by then that saying yes to God is very rarely about self-promotion. More often, saying yes to God means agreeing to an assignment where the line of people willing to accomplish it is pretty short.

There are long lines of young men and women wanting to plant churches. And I felt sure that the churches in Scottsdale and Fort Lauderdale had received scores of resumes from folks interested in filling those slots. But the list of people begging to come to New Life and rebuild all that had been tragically broken? I envisioned that line being very, very short. And I imagined that God was asking me to stand at the front of it.

In my heart of hearts, I knew what I needed to do. "Lord," I said, "if you call me here, I will say yes." I heard nothing in response, but I knew the deal had been sealed.

The pastoral search committee at New Life whittled their final four to a single finalist in a matter of days, but it was at least a week before I received word that I was the guy. It was during those in-between days that the Lord spoke to me during a few minutes of quiet time in my office back at Gateway Church one morning. Although inaudibly, I sensed him say, *Brady, they're going to choose you.*

Given the exchange he and I had shared in that Colorado Springs hotel, the news came as no surprise to me. My only lingering curiosity was about whether God would prepare Pam's heart for this move as he so graciously had worked to prepare mine. My curiosity wouldn't last long: less than one hour later my phone rang, and it was Pam. "We're going to Colorado Springs," I think were her words exactly.

As she was packing up our house that morning, having no idea whether the destination for our move would involve the Southeast, the Mountain West, or somewhere in between, God had given her specific insight that Colorado Springs would be our new home.

I said, "Honey, it's amazing that you're saying this, because about an hour ago the Lord said to me that New Life was going to choose me to serve as their new senior pastor."

Several days later my friend Tom Lane, who serves as executive senior pastor at Gateway Church, called and said, "Someone gave me a gift certificate to the Silver Fox, and it's enough for four. You and Pam interested in joining us tomorrow night?"

It was short notice, but the Silver Fox is one of Dallas's finest steakhouses, and I'm a big fan of steak. "We're in," I said.

The next night, Tom and his wife swung by to pick up Pam and me. Curiously, Tom didn't take the direct route to the restaurant. After twenty minutes or so, the four of us were parked on a street miles from our destination, near the site of a church under construction. "Hey," Tom said to me. "What do you think of that building—the aesthetics and everything?"

I looked out the passenger-side window and saw a very plain, very industrial-looking facade in the distance. "I don't know," I said. "I guess I don't think much of it. I mean, *look* at it."

Tom stared at it for a while, until I finally asked, "Why are we sitting on the side of a road, staring at a church building in the middle of nowhere, when we could be eating steaks?"

He mumbled incoherently in reply and slowly pulled away.

We finally got to the Silver Fox—late for our reservation, of course, since we had taken time to go stare at the ugly church building—and I quickly discovered that Tom had reserved a private room off to the side of the main dining room. I had seen it before and knew it was a comfortable room, but it was the type of place you'd request if you were entertaining a large group, not a party of four. I asked Tom about it, and he replied, "Oh, I don't know. I guess I thought it would be kind of cool to hang out just us couples and to have a quiet place to talk."

Whatever you say, Tom. Just point me to my steak.

We walked over to the doors that led to the private room, and as Tom opened them, I caught sight of two of New Life's search committee members and their wives. In unison, Lance and Rachel Coles and Brian and Pam Newberg said, "Surprise!"

I'm sure my face betrayed how shocked I was. "What are you guys doing here?" I asked.

"We flew to Dallas tonight to let you know that you are the man we want as the new senior pastor of New Life Church."

I was incredibly humbled—and finally onto Tom. I quickly learned that the reason for our random detour was that the Coleses' and New-bergs' flight had been delayed. Tom was forced to punt so the surprise could be preserved.

That evening at the Silver Fox was fantastic. We laughed together, cried together, and, thankfully, ate some really good steak. We recounted how the entire search process had unfolded, and logged our hopes and dreams for the future. It was a confirming evening, an evening that told me that for reasons I didn't fully understand, I was supposed to serve at New Life Church.

Afterward another surprise awaited us. Pam and I were led to another couple's home, where inside, the Gateway elders and their wives had gathered for dessert and coffee — and to celebrate that New Life had selected me to serve.

God had spoken clearly to me and then to Pam. God had spoken to New Life's search committee. And the elders from Gateway were gracious in their willingness to release me to serve in a new capacity. It was a wonderful night. But the journey was just beginning, and it would prove more challenging than even I could have imagined.

During the roughest patches after the shooting, I would think back on the day those same elders — along with the overseers from New Life — laid hands on my wife and me and prayed for us during my installation service as senior pastor at my new church home. I had done ministry with those men and I had done life with them. We had laughed together, cried together, prayed together, endured arguments together, and still loved each other deeply. As I knelt at the altar there in Colorado Springs, it occurred to me that you don't make old friends overnight. It takes time. Years. Decades even. During my darkest days, I remembered that scene and thought, "I'm not in this alone." True, I *felt* alone. But I wasn't. I had spiritual fathers and old friends committed to staying by my side. Nobody survives tragedy alone. Because of their presence in my life, I knew I'd make it through.

* * *

My first Sunday to speak at New Life Church as the official senior pastor finalist was on August 12, 2007, which also happened to be Pam's and my eighteenth wedding anniversary. It would be the first installment in a three-weekend audition of sorts, in which I would preach on the topics of my choosing and then be subjected to a congregational vote the following week. Although the search committee had chosen me, the congregation still had to approve their choice.

I knew a few friends who had gone through a church voting process, and from what I had observed, it was brutal at best. As I walked through my own three-week trial, I felt like I had a giant placard slung around my neck that read, "Will preach for food." It was horrible, but only because I had never been "voted on" for anything in my life. I had been prayed over, selected, and appointed. But never *voted* into a ministry role. The experience was not unlike a Christian version of *American Idol* mixed with *Survivor*, except that there was no million-dollar prize at the end.

Finally, on Sunday, September 2, 2007, after a successful congregational vote had come and gone, I was able to take the platform, place my Bible on the podium, approach the microphone, and say, "Good morning! I'm Brady Boyd, and I'm your new senior pastor."

Prior to coming to New Life, I had been told by my friend Clark Whitten, who took the reins of a megachurch in Oklahoma after the founding pastor was asked to step down, that I would encounter three groups of people upon arriving at New Life Church. The first group, Clark said, would trust me immediately because they are trusting people, and trusting people trust their pastor. The second group would *want* to trust me but would make me wait awhile before they would consent to doing so, mostly because of the hurt they'd experienced in the past. And then there would be a third group, who *never* would trust me, no matter what I said or did. Actually, they'd probably never trust another senior pastor, period. They had been too wounded, too deceived, too blindsided by past experiences. And they certainly weren't going to risk getting their hearts broken that way again.

Whenever I preached at Gateway, which was typically half a dozen times a year, I could look out at the congregation and in every single area see faces of people I knew. I knew their name; I knew their spouse's name; I knew where they worked; I knew the ages of their kids. I had performed their marriage or buried their grandmother. There was real relationship there, and as a result it was a joy to preach. But at New Life, I knew nobody. Save for the members of the search committee and their spouses, everyone was a stranger. And those first few months as I preached, I would look out at the crowd and see Clark's three-category theory playing out in spades. "There's a one," I would think. "There's a two. And that guy for *sure* is a three."

I felt the same way on those post-shooting days when I would deliver a press conference. As I would convey the facts as best as I understood them, I'd think, "I need for the congregation to believe that what I am telling them is the truth."

In his grace, God reminded me in the midst of the tumult that I had signed up for a marathon, not a sprint. It would take some time for me to restore credibility to the senior pastor's role. While I had not done anything to lose credibility personally, the role I was filling there was tainted. And I knew that well. During those first few lonely weeks, I estimated it would take me about five full years to garner deep trust from the majority of the congregation. I'm at the halfway point today, and I stand by that initial guess.

Without a doubt, the departure from Gateway and arrival at New Life has been the most significant transition I've ever known. There have been other life changes that make my top-ten list, but none that would affect every level of my life as deeply as has this one.

Some of my earliest memories as a little boy in northwest Louisiana are of church. My mom, especially, was a very devout Christian and an even more devout churchgoer. If the doors were open, we were there, unless someone in the Boyd family was injured or ill.

The routine would have been fine by me, except that there always seemed to be trouble around the church. It wasn't a place of peace, a fact that even a grade-school kid could pick up on. Though I didn't have the vocabulary to articulate it at the time, I knew there were strong political factions within that congregation, and being around that much infighting can wear a young guy out.

When I was ten or eleven years old, a pastor was voted in at our church. Two years later he suddenly was asked to leave. Some man who held a position of authority among the congregation stood up, took another vote, counted raised hands, and said in essence, "He's out."

To my knowledge, there was no real reason for our pastor's ousting. Still, hours after the decision was made, that man and his wife had to pack up their house, load up their kids, and head out of town. There were no goodbyes or explanations. He had been my pastor, but in the blink of a vote he was gone.

That same awful scenario happened twice in my young life, and after the second occurrence, I made a vow to God that I would be anything in life he wanted me to be, as long as that something was *not* a pastor. Who in his right mind wanted to work hard for years and years, only to be summarily dismissed and ushered out of town? No, thanks.

When, in my late teens, I finally did feel the tug of God's call to vocational ministry, I thought he was mad at me. I had intentionally gone to a secular college and worked toward a secular degree so God would be clear that I was cut out for journalism and not for church work, but I see now that he had other things in mind.

My first pastoral assignment was with a large church. It was a good church, but the stimulating, high-challenge environment was nearly my undoing. At the end of four years of my working eighty-hour weeks, Pam was ready to call it quits on our marriage. Fearing that the only person who truly mattered to me was about to walk away, I said, "Pam, I'll resign tomorrow. Just, please, don't leave."

I kept my word, handed in my letter of resignation, and dove headlong back into business. I worked at a radio station and then at a TV station, where I forged a path into senior management. By that time, I was receiving offers to come manage stations in smaller markets, which is exactly what I thought I'd spend the rest of my life doing. I pushed harder and harder in that world, believing that if I could assemble a strong track record of success in media, God would lay off the pastor track.

But then came Amarillo.

I was working in Shreveport, Louisiana, when the offer surfaced for me to become the sales manager for a media company in Amarillo, Texas. The company owned two radio stations that weren't thriving, and they believed I might be the catalyst they needed to turn things around.

Later that day, after I explained the opportunity to Pam, she and I tried to locate Amarillo on a map. If only Google Earth had existed back then: we studied the Texas map in our road atlas for several minutes before finally figuring out that because the state was so big, the mapmaker had put the entire panhandle on a separate page. Flipping over the sheet that bore three-quarters of our new state, at last we located Amarillo. Evidently, we would be leaving the tiny north woods of Louisiana for the wild, wild West.

It is now obvious to Pam and me both that God had at least two reasons for sending us to Texas. It was in Amarillo that we would adopt our wonderful children, Abram and Callie. And it was there that we would find Trinity Fellowship Church, the place that restored my belief in the existence of "healthy church."

Days after our move to Amarillo, Pam and I were pointed toward Trinity by some new acquaintances. It was a church of several thousand people, but they had a small singles' group. One of the staff leaders somehow learned that I had previously served as a pastor, and one Sunday after services, he mentioned that the singles' group leader had just moved away. "Would you be willing to teach the class next Sunday morning?" he asked.

It was only a volunteer deal, and a short-term one at that. But still, my nerves were wracked. I had decided to stay away from all forms of church work and preferred to simply attend services on Sunday. Again, God had his own ideas.

I said yes to the opportunity but very quickly regretted it. "I've done it again," I thought. "I've just roped myself back into the slavery known as ministry."

That Sunday morning, I stepped into the appointed classroom to find exactly six people inside. I thought, "Cool. I can do this. Six people is the perfect size for my commitment level."

Six months later I was still volunteering short-term, more than one hundred people were attending the class on a regular basis, and I was annoyed. The last thing I wanted was to be successful in a ministry capacity. I wanted to be successful in *business*. I didn't want to be a pastor. I wanted to keep my life and my marriage intact. I wanted to live free. But I couldn't deny that Trinity Fellowship was healthy and that despite my regular service for six months straight, I still felt whole as a person, a husband, and a Christ follower. What was I to do with *that*?

As a singles' group, we grew until eventually we were forced to break into several smaller groups that could then reproduce themselves. Once I backfilled my leadership role, another church in west Texas — this one in Hereford — called and asked if I would come fill in for them on Sunday mornings. Their senior pastor had left, and they needed someone who wasn't intimidated by a pulpit to come teach them the Bible. I was intrigued, but I still had a full-time job in media. I wasn't sure how this would work, but I was willing to give it a try.

Pam and I drove to Hereford the following Sunday morning, and I taught that little congregation with energy to spare. From there, our weekend ritual was waking early on Sunday mornings, gathering up our new baby boy, Abram, and making the forty-mile drive to Hereford. I would preach the morning message, we would eat lunch at a nearby café, and then we would make the forty-mile trek back home. It lacked fanfare, but it was *important* work. I knew it then and recognize it still today.

Six months into our Hereford experience, even if in defiance of my deepest, most sincere prayers, the church began to grow. The leaders came to me and said, "Brady, would you come be our pastor?" I was torn by the question. Everything I had done in the world of church work while in Texas was in a volunteer capacity, which meant I could quit at any time. Plus, the church's offer was a whopping thirty grand a year less than what I was making in the media industry. Did I really want to reenslave myself, and for pennies on the dollar? And don't get me started on our need to relocate to Hereford, a town where the cow-to-person ratio hovers at fifteen to one even today.

Still, I felt — dare I say — *called.* And given my experience at Trinity, I believed for the first time in my life that the church could be a whole and holy people, a group who actually practiced what Scripture preached. Suffice it to say, in the fall of 1998 I gladly became the senior pastor of Trinity Fellowship Church (no relationship to the Trinity from which I had just come) in Hereford, Texas. We would grow from fifty to two hundred in the space of a couple of years, and I would learn valuable lessons about what a church can look like when integrity rules the day. After three wonderful years in Hereford, Pam and I would then accept the opportunity to help plant Gateway Church. And from there, New Life.

I pray my most significant departures are behind me. I really do. In fact, I have made a personal pact to never again say, "Oh, God, I'm bored — please give me a bigger challenge," which is basically the prayer that ushered in every major life transition I have known. As my story proves, sometimes God takes a guy up on that prayer. And sometimes the ensuing challenge is bigger than what he ever would knowingly accept.

* * *

First Kings 1:28–52 recounts the story of David turning over his leadership reins to his son Solomon. I've always been fascinated by this particular event in Scripture because of the fact that of all the sons David could have chosen, he selected one who was the product of his adulterous affair with Bathsheba. I wonder if Solomon was sort of pushed aside throughout his childhood because he was a tangible reminder of such a terrible season in King David's life. But as David neared death and needed a successor to the throne, he looked directly at Solomon and in essence said, "You're the one."

Over the years, I have developed a theory about why Solomon was selected. Despite the details surrounding his entrance into the world, I believe the reason he was tapped to lead a nation was that he had caught the DNA of his father, who had a willing heart, a willing spirit, and an honest desire to serve. Granted, David had faced his own share of challenges along the way. But in the end, he would be called a man after God's own heart. He was a leader whom God could *trust*.

I look at the legacy of guys like David and Solomon and feel the pull of healthy covetousness. How I crave a legacy like that. I don't care if I am ever known for my teaching and preaching, for my talents and gifts, for my list of earthly successes, whatever they may be. I want to be known as a wise man—a man after God's own heart. If there was one thing I would need in the days immediately following the shooting, it was the manifested presence of my heavenly Father's DNA: strength and integrity, calmness and a sense of peace, wisdom and perseverance, kindness and an insistence that though all around feels unbearably dark, hope—*true* hope—still abounds.

CHAPTER 3

Enduring
Death's Valley

God is the only one who can make
the valley of trouble a door of hope.
— *Catherine Marshall*

A FEW MONTHS AFTER PAM, THE KIDS, AND I MOVED FROM TEXAS TO Colorado, we purchased a house in northern Colorado Springs a few miles from the church. It was going to be the perfect spot for us, a nice piece of property with lots of trees and grass and a great view of mesas out to the east. But the first few days in that home, I realized that I wasn't quite accustomed to all the nooks and crannies just yet.

I would get up in the middle of the night to get a drink of water or visit the restroom, and not wanting to wake Pam by flipping on the light, I'd try to navigate the path in the dark. But I hadn't memorized the contour of the walls. I didn't know how many steps it was from my bed to the bathroom. I hadn't figured out how to read shadows through the windows and use them as night-lights in those first few days. And inevitably I'd stub my toe.

It made me feel incredibly vulnerable to be unable to navigate my own house. Vulnerable and foolish—I mean, how hard is it to get to a room that is ten feet away? But darkness threatens our confidence and does its best to squelch our faith. When there is no light to be found, we feel alone, unsure, and weak.

The Tuesday following the shooting, as I sat in the dim, pre-sunrise light of my office, I was tempted to feel like that. The immediacy of the horrible event had passed, and for the first time since it happened, I was left alone with my thoughts. For a fleeting moment, I considered buying the lie that the darkness which had been present that Sunday would remain with me—with us as a church—forever. I considered handing over my confidence, my sure-footedness, my faith, and giving in to the darkness instead.

But as I say, the moment didn't stick around. Thankfully, those lesser thoughts were quickly evicted by the truth of God's powerful Word.

When I was a kid in Sunday school, I memorized the well-known verses from Psalm 23, and I have read the psalm scores of times throughout my life. But that passage of Scripture wouldn't come to life for me until Tuesday morning, December 11. On that day, the words were no longer theory. They were for me a *rhema*, Greek for a timely word spoken by the Spirit of God that perfectly addresses the situation at hand.

"The LORD is my shepherd," those six verses begin, "I shall not be in want. He makes me lie down in green pastures, he leads me beside quiet waters, he restores my soul. He guides me in paths of righteousness for his name's sake.

"Even though I walk through the valley of the shadow of death, I will fear no evil, for you are with me; your rod and your staff, they comfort me. You prepare a table before me in the presence of my enemies. You anoint my head with oil; my cup overflows. Surely goodness and love will follow me all the days of my life, and I will dwell in the house of the LORD forever."

In the early-morning hours of that Tuesday, it was the first part of verse 4 that stopped me short. "Even though I walk through the valley of the shadow of death," it says, "I will fear no evil, for you are with me." I thought about the valley of the shadow of death that our people were walking through, and how those periods of darkness can strike when least expected in life. Clearly, they can come when a loved one is snatched from your presence, as the Works girls were from their family and our congregation. But they can also surface in more subtle ways.

Throughout years of pastoral ministry, I have watched people wrestle with occupational darkness, behavioral darkness, marital darkness, parenting darkness, the darkness of depression, and more. I have seen faithful followers of Christ battle unexplained long-term illness, wage war against a mountain of debt that looms over them, and stand firm against spiritual forces that daily threaten to take them out.

And it's into *all* such darkness that you and I face that God's Word speaks.

If there is anyone in Scripture qualified to offer up instruction when it comes to dealing effectively with darkness, it is King David. He spent a good deal of time trudging through valleys, I think you'd agree. He was at times a lousy husband, a mediocre father, and a dysfunctional leader. But through it all, something remained pure inside this man, something that God would choose to redeem. He would allow David to leave a worthwhile legacy, which includes the verses of Psalm 23. And if there was anything helpful to be gleaned from those words, I craved it that Tuesday morning as I read my Bible.

I first homed in on one single word. "Though I walk *through* the valley of the shadow of death..." I could see that David endured a dark time. But I could also see that he was never going to pitch his tent there; he was moving *through* it. That's what I needed to do now.

I knew that the Bible never promises us valley-free living. It's the opposite, really. The apostle James speaks candidly about *when* we will face trials, not *if*, and I was convinced New Life would continue to face their fair share of despair. But those episodes don't have to define us; they don't have to constitute the place we call home. David knew in his heart that although the darkness would descend on him, he was not called to dwell in it permanently. There is a time to weep and mourn and grieve, as Ecclesiastes 3 says. But there also is a time to laugh and sing and dance. The time comes when we must move on.

In essence, I felt David was saying, "I am walking through the valley of the shadow of death, but I know that eventually this dismal landscape will give way to a mountaintop on the other side." He made up his mind on dark day number one that he would keep walking, planting one foot in front of the other, until the mountain came into view. The journey may have taken him an hour, a day, or a decade, but he was convinced it would lead to something good. Someday the sun was going to shine again. Someday he'd bid that valley farewell.

I will laugh again, I imagined David thinking.

I will dance once more.

I will celebrate sometime in the future.

This is not the end of my joy.

I'm in a valley to beat all valleys here, but there's a mountaintop on the other side.

The biggest lie that the enemy of our souls will serve up during times of darkness is that *there is no mountaintop*. He schemes and strategizes to convince us that we'll never again see the light of day, so we should just settle in for the long haul. Satan slithers up to us during a tough time and sneers, "What you fear is true: you'll never get out of this ordeal in one piece, so why bother even trying? See everyone around you laughing and dancing and enjoying life? That will never be you again. You are not going to make it through this valley. This, I'm afraid, is *home*."

Those words seem altogether true for those stuck in a marriage on the rocks. They seem true for the one staring down that growing pile of debt. And they seemed true for us at New Life on the heels of December 9. The biggest lie we had to expose and then fervently refute was the one that threatened our hope. We had to remind each other that even though we didn't know how to read these new shadows just yet, our frustrating stubbed-toe nights would one day come to an end. Despite the present surroundings in our lives, it wouldn't always be dark.

Psalm 23 continues with a declaration from David when he found himself in the dark. "Though I walk through the valley of the shadow of death," he says, *"I will fear no evil"* (Ps. 23:4, emphasis added).

I don't know exactly what type of evil David was referring to, but I know the type I encountered the day of the shooting. Evil was made manifest right before me, in a manner I'd never seen before. Figuratively and literally, Satan wanted to kill those of us at New Life Church that day. Using a young man's guns, our enemy planned to bring us down. And in my heart, as gunfire erupted in that first-floor hallway, I knew he might just succeed.

We are in a real battle, and Satan plays for keeps. It's not merely a philosophical battle, a theological battle, a battle of wits. The fight is also *visceral*, one that can hit you right in the gut. But the victory already is God's. I took great comfort in that reality that day.

I've been asked over the past three years how I would characterize the evil that I sensed at work when Matthew Murray entered our campus, and in response I have explained that it felt as if an ominous cloud had appeared on the horizon and was racing its way toward our church. A wave of unmistakable darkness was preparing to engulf us, and spiritually that darkness felt all too real. What's more, thwarting its progress seemed about as futile as trying to stop a storm. During such times, it often seems that the best you can hope for is to find shelter—a safe place to just wait it out.

The context for New Life's storm was that after the brief, thirteen-month period following the scandal involving Ted Haggard, we were about to be on the front page of every major newspaper in the country for a second time, and for reasons that were again anything but pleasant. It was like getting knocked to your knees by a heavyweight fighter and then feeling the impact of a sweeping, right-hand punch that lands squarely on your jaw — you have no recourse but to fall flat to the mat.

Flat on the mat for the full ten-count — that was Satan's earnest desire for New Life Church that day. And it was hard not to cave to his scheme. One of our longtime worship leaders, Jon Egan, felt hopeless during those days. "I think we're done," he said of our situation. "I really think that we're done."

Within days, Jon's hope would be restored as God whispered assurances that as a church we would pull through, but for then, I understood what he meant. From an earthly perspective, all indications were that our best days as a church were behind us. I also knew that while I'd had to endure only one punch at New Life, Jon had suffered two. He had been on staff the year before, when things exploded the first time around. He had still been on his knees, gasping for air, trying to make sense of his pastor's untimely departure, when the shooting occurred. How was he supposed to recover now? The second punch had connected, and the prospect of brighter days seemed a cruel illusion at best.

Thankfully, God had in mind a plan for helping us all rise again.

Should we fear the evil that could present itself, as it did on December 9? I've been asked that by others since the tragedy. Actually, I've asked the question myself, and my answer always leads me back to one of my favorite stories in Scripture, which is found in Luke 10. There we discover that Jesus, the greatest leader ever to walk the planet, had taken a group of men to be at his side as he ministered here on earth — seventy-two, to be exact. He performed miracles in front of them, he showed them firsthand how to exhibit the fruit of the Spirit

—traits such as love and joy, peace and patience, kindness and goodness, and so forth—and he trained them to point others toward the
type of faith that would save their souls.

Then one day the fearless leader decided it was time to send his
followers out into the world and see what they could do on their own.
According to Luke 10:3, he said, "On your way! But be careful—this
is hazardous work. You're like lambs in a wolf pack" (MSG).

It fell a little short of a reassuring send-off, if you ask me.

I imagine they were terrified. Raising the dead and casting out
demons and performing miracles left and right had all looked so easy
for Jesus. But now he was leaving them to their own devices? They,
who had never done *anything* like that before?

But off they went. And upon returning from their grand adventure,
instead of showing up with scared-stiff countenances, the seventy-two
were bubbling over with exciting reports to share. They came back
"with joy," verse 17 says. The source of all their enthusiasm was that,
according to them, even the *demons* had submitted to Jesus' name.

Without intending to, those disciples had revealed the core of their
theological belief. They believed that the forces at work in the universe included one very big God and one very big Devil. Big God,
big Devil—those were the players they saw. They had encountered
some of big Devil's minions and were overjoyed that those demons
had retreated in Jesus' name.

I imagine Jesus shaking his head the entire time his valiant men
relayed their eager update. "No, no, no," I picture him saying. "Boys,
your theology is way, way off."

Jesus then says to his disciples and to us, "I saw Satan fall like lightning from heaven. I have given you authority to trample on snakes
and scorpions and to overcome all the power of the enemy; *nothing*
will harm you. However, do not rejoice that the spirits submit to you,
but rejoice that your names are written in heaven" (Luke 10:18–20,
emphasis added).

"Quit making such a big deal out of the demons submitting to you," he essentially said that day. "Quit fearing evil! Instead, rejoice that your heart belongs to God!"

The book of Isaiah says that Satan fell from heaven and took one-third of the angelic host with him. But it is here in this passage in Luke that the blanks are filled in regarding what that eviction entailed. In short, it was a very quick fight.

I'm not sure if you've ever been in a fistfight, but I'm sad to say that I had my fair share of them during my childish, growing-up days. And each and every time, the scrawny-kid version of me fell precisely "like lightning" to the ground. I may have thought I was putting up a good fight, but the odds *never* were on my side.

It was the same where Satan was concerned. When he decided to go toe-to-toe with God, he instantly sealed his fate. "Your theology accounts for a big God and a big Devil," I imagine Jesus explaining that day to the seventy-two who had returned triumphant and proud. "But in fact only one of them is 'big.' Big God, way-small Devil—*that's* the theology to embrace."

Think about this with me: Because of Satan's defiance, in one fell swoop heaven lost a third of its staff overnight. If that happened in any corporation in America, that company would be hamstrung for quite some time. But nowhere in Scripture do I read of a recession in heaven after that massive layoff.

God did not stop being God just because a third of his team got thrown out. In fact, I believe God was *equally* as powerful on the day after their departure as he was on the days when they were there. Of *course* God was. It is impossible for God to change. And it is this God who upholds us when we face our darkest days.

I've been a fan of the Discovery Channel's TV show *MythBusters* for a few years now. One hour a week, two geeky but very entertaining guys named Adam and Jamie orchestrate elaborate experiments to validate or challenge common myths, such as the one about Jimmy Hoffa's body being buried in the concrete underneath Giants Stadium, or the color red having the ability to drive a bull toward psychopathy, or whether it was possible for the 1962 escapees from Alcatraz who went missing without a trace to have survived the tides of San Francisco Bay in a homemade raft.

Not long ago Adam and Jamie devoted an entire episode to proving or disproving whether elephants really are scared of mice. The guys stuck a little white mouse underneath a bowl that was rigged to a wire and then placed that bowl in the path of a small herd of elephants. As the herd approached, Adam and Jamie yanked on the wire, which flipped the bowl upside down and revealed the innocent rodent, and the elephants immediately scattered—presumably out of fear.

It seemed to validate the myth, except that what if it was merely the movement of the bowl—and not the mouse itself—that frightened the herd? Adam and Jamie adjusted the experiment and gave it a second try. This time they took the mouse away and had the herd approach a bowl that had nothing hidden underneath. As the elephants neared, they tugged on the wire, flipped the bowl over, and watched in amazement as the huge creatures charged on by.

Elephants really *do* fear mice, as ludicrous as that seems.

Which makes me wonder what you and I must look like, both to the angels assembled in heaven and to the God they live to serve. I wonder if we bear resemblance to the classic circus elephant poised awkwardly atop a small stool. With one single step, the giant beast weighing several tons could crush a tiny mouse, and yet it cowers in fear, forgetting the strength that lies within.

Listen, you and I must be diligent to see ourselves as protected and sustained by our unmatched and unchanging King. Everything is under his authority. *Everything*—stage-four cancer, the economy, the marriage that struggles to survive. No matter the circumstance you face, it is no reason to live nervously up on that stool. God defeated Satan himself, he defeated death on the cross, and he promises that ultimate victory can be ours when the worlds of good and evil once and for all collide. This was part of God's you-will-rise-again plan for New Life Church, and it is part of his plan for you too.

Why, then, should we fear any evil? Evil cannot win.

When Jesus' disciples returned from their seemingly victorious outing and boasted of having overcome a sizable dose of evil in the world, he directed them to the matter of their own hearts. It was as if he were saying, "Sure, it's great that you commanded a few demons to submit to you, but that is *nothing* compared with the battle you've already won. The biggest battle you will ever face in life is the one that rages in your own hearts. It is not the external battles that threaten to take down most people but the *inside job* that gets them every time. It's the war between a human being and his or her own proneness to stay forever enslaved to sin that you have to watch out for. That's the bloodiest war of all."

I don't know what type of evil you have encountered thus far in this journey called life, but this much I am sure of: if you are a follower of Jesus Christ, you are guaranteed victory in the end. By the presence of his Holy Spirit, you are destined to overcome. Satan's schemes and strategies for you will ultimately fail, unless you choose to give them entry into your heart.

Think of your life as a well-engineered ocean liner cruising along on the high seas. Because of the integrity in the ship's manufacturing process, the only way that liner will go down is if water somehow gets inside.

Surrounding the boat are billions of gallons of water, representing the fallen world in which you and I live. Sometimes the ride is as smooth as glass, but if you live life long enough, you'll find your share of choppy, tumultuous waves that make you want to cough up your lunch. But even in those dreadful conditions, the only way you'll sink is if that evil is allowed inside.

It is possible to weather the most intense storms of life without allowing our hearts to be wrecked. It is possible to cut through vicious waters without allowing bitterness and rage to have their way. It is possible to stay afloat on rough seas without letting something like unforgiveness take us out.

But we first must learn to lean into the never-failing presence of God.

My daughter, Callie, loves to play baseball, and recently her baseball coach asked her what she wants to be when she grows up. Without missing a beat, she replied, "A horse jockey." Which tells me that Pam and I had better start saving our pennies for a pony.

Another kid Callie's age answered the question this way: "I want to be a lion tamer." He said, "I want to go inside a giant cage that is just *full* of lions. I want to snap my big whip and make them do whatever I say to do!"

Obviously fascinated by the sound of his own voice, he kept going. "And I'm not talking about *small* lions," he explained passionately. "I'm talking about those big, hairy ones. The ones with wild manes and huge, pointed teeth and a roar that makes the whole *world* shake!"

The little boy continued on, detailing every aspect of his one-day profession until it finally occurred to him that the dream he was describing was quite a dangerous one to pursue. The more he talked, the more he realized that the job might be a bit bigger than he was capable of handling, which is why at the end of his zeal-filled spiel, he said, "But of course, my mommy will be with me."

I don't know about you, but there are plenty of times in my life when I have wished it was socially acceptable for a fortysomething married man who is the father of two to request his mommy's presence. *Plenty* of times. Life doesn't seem quite as threatening when someone stronger and more experienced is around.

The most vivid example of this truth playing out in my life occurred when I was still a kid. Growing up, I was a small boy — frail even. By high school I began to fill out, but in grade school and middle school I had a slight build and was therefore the perfect target for bullying. I was picked on frequently, and to make matters worse, the schools I attended were staffed by teachers and principals utterly oblivious to the unruly goings-on of the kids in their care.

My family had moved from northwest Louisiana to east Texas early in my grade school years, and while I did make friends along the way, I still attracted my share of enemies. Fast-forward to my freshman year of high school, when I had made the baseball team and was the only freshman selected to be a starter. Which was great news, except that evidently I took the center-field roster spot of a guy who had really big friends.

That group of big friends decided one day to tie me up, coil a thick rope around my neck, and drag me by that rope up a steep hill. It was "just a little hazing," as they put it, for knocking their buddy off the team. That little bit of hazing almost took my life.

When I got home later that afternoon, I yanked on a shirt that would hide the burns on my neck. The last thing I wanted was for my dad to see what had happened to his son. My dad was a real man's man — what kid wanted his strong, steady father to find out that he couldn't defend himself against a few thugs?

That night, after I'd taken my shower, I came out of the bathroom with a normal T-shirt on. I was headed for bed, but I didn't make it there before my brother noticed my bruised and cut-up neck and raced off to tell my dad that something had happened to me that day. Dad called me into the living room, where I had to explain the afternoon's events and show him the severity of the injuries I had sustained. I'm not sure which was more humiliating: being dragged up the hill by those bullies or having to tell the man I most admired the painful, ugly truth.

The next morning, I woke, got ready for school, and was on my way out the door, when my dad said, "Brady, you're not going to school just yet. You can head up there this afternoon, but for the next few hours, I'd like you to stay here."

I later would learn that en route to his job at the local ConAgra Foods plant, my dad had paid a visit to my school. To this day, I have no idea what transpired, but given that my dad's life wasn't surrendered to Jesus Christ quite yet and that he could be something of a fireball when the mood was right, I imagine the conversation was quite colorful. And brief.

As instructed, I arrived at school several hours later and immediately was approached by both my high school principal and my baseball coach. "Nothing like this *ever* will happen again," they assured me with sincere eyes and intensity in their voices. And from that day until the day I graduated from high school, I never was picked on again.

I learned two key things as a result of that terrible incident. First, I learned that I have a very low tolerance for bullies. Now that I am a grown man who is no longer small and frail, I find that whenever I encounter bullying of any type, something inside me erupts. This is especially true if the bully's target is my wife, one of my kids, or someone on New Life's staff. If someone I dearly love is being mistreated or pushed around, I just can't help but respond. And so immediately after Matthew Murray's rampage, I remember thinking, "You are not going to win this fight, Satan. I *refuse* to let a bully like you win."

Second, I learned that it pays to keep your dad close by. The reality is this: if my father had been standing beside his high school son on the hillside that day in east Texas, there is no way those boys would have gone through with their plan. Of course, my dad *wasn't* there, but he did show up for me as soon as I allowed him into my situation. And because of his little chat with the school officials, I felt protected that day. Many kids may not know what that feels like, to have a parent defend them to that degree, but I do. My earthly father defended me well, which made it easier for me to envision a heavenly Father having my back.

You probably know where I am going with this. I'm going exactly where King David went, back in the Twenty-third Psalm. The last part of verse 4 says that the reason David could walk through the valley of the shadow of death, the reason he could fear no evil, is that his God was *with him*.

"Even though I walk through the valley of the shadow of death, I will fear no evil, for you are with me."

Almighty, all-powerful God with us—is there a more wonderful promise than that?

From countless conversations I have had over the years with Christ followers of every age and every conceivable background, I realize it is possible that you have known your share of death in this life. You may have been forced to say an agonizing farewell to a baby who would never be born. You may have lost your financial footing and watched as every semblance of your earthly security died. Maybe it was the death of a job or of a parent or of a marriage in which you once found great joy. It could have been the death of your physical health or the death of a long-held dream. Whatever death you have known in your life, God has been present each step of the way.

What's more, if you sense you're walking through one of those shadowy valleys even today, rest assured that he remains with you now. This life is undeniably fraught with uncertainty, mystery, and risk. Not all of that is bad, but carrying too big a bucket of what-ifs can really weigh a person down. If you're walking through a dark season, ask God to remind you that he is near. Request his divine strength to keep planting one foot in front of the other, and his divine power to help keep evil at bay.

God answered those prayers for me, two days after the shooting. And because he loves to show up in strength and power, I'm confident he'll do the same for you.

First Samuel 17 tells the story of the teenage version of the psalmist David trying to talk King Saul into letting him charge into battle and take out the infamous giant Goliath, who for more than a month had been taunting the Israelites and mocking their God. The stakes of Saul's decision were sky-high; whoever won in the fight against Goliath would claim victory for the entire battle. And David thought Saul would be wise to send a mere boy to accomplish this feat? He had a tough sales job in front of him.

In an effort to persuade the king, David began to rattle off his resumé. Here is what he said: "Your servant has been keeping his father's sheep. When a lion or a bear came and carried off a sheep from the flock, I went after it, struck it and rescued the sheep from its mouth" (1 Sam. 17:34–35).

Allow me to push "pause" on David's speech for a second. Clearly, I am no parks-and-wildlife expert, but this much I know: when a bear has food in its mouth, it is best not to attempt to remove it. This is a helpful piece of advice, don't you think?

But David never once followed it.

"When it turned on me," he continued, as if it were a shocking turn of events for a provoked bear to fight back, "I seized it by its hair, struck it and killed it" (1 Sam. 17:35).

It's important to note here that David wasn't referring to a mere bear cub. He was talking about a *mature* bear that he killed with his own two hands. And his slingshot, I suppose.

Every time I read about David's courageous feats in the wild, I imagine what the other sheep in the flock thought when they saw their shepherd take down a wild, angry bear. I happen to believe that they comprised the most trash-talking bunch of sheep around. I envision them sauntering up to lions and tigers and bears all over their neighborhood, saying, "You see what just happened to your buddy, Frank? Mm-h'mmm. That's *our* shepherd, boys! You want a piece of the action? Huh? You want some of this?"

In far more reverent ways, this is exactly how I feel when I walk through life with God. As I take each step of the journey by his side, I consider what he has done to those throughout history who have tried to mock him; and to Satan and all of his evil demons, I whisper, "Hey, boys. You want some of this?"

My friend, this is the same way you have to envision yourself. The God of all creation is flanking you on the left and on the right. He has gone before you, he promises to stay the course with you, and he has your back like nobody here on earth can. Our Shepherd — the Good Shepherd, our God — is the only one who can help us find the mountaintop when we are stumbling through the dark. There *is* a mountaintop, I assure you. But sometimes that long-awaited peak can be appreciated only when it is found as a result of enduring the valley first.

Not long after that tragic week of December 2007, I received word one Sunday morning that a nineteen-month-old girl in our community had been accidentally run over by her father, who was backing his truck out of the driveway. Unbeknownst to him, the toddler was playing a few feet behind him, and in the blink of an eye her little body had borne the full impact of a several-ton vehicle.

The girl and her family were close friends of a family who are part of our church, and on that tragic Sunday morning, during the junior high worship service one of our students received a text on his phone from his dad, alerting him that the close family friend had been run over and was being rushed to the hospital. "She may die within the hour," the screen read.

Aaron, the junior high student, rushed up to one of our youth pastors, Jared Newman, told him of the incident, and frantically asked, "What should I do? What do we do?"

Pastor Jared looked into the eyes of a terrified middle-schooler and said, "Aaron, do you believe that God can heal?"

"Absolutely," Aaron replied, his voice suddenly strong and steady.

"Do you believe that God's promises are still relevant today?" Pastor Jared then asked.

"Yes!" Aaron said.

"Then you go to that child right now. Get your stuff. Get to the hospital. Lay hands on that little girl. And ask that God would heal her today."

Pastor Jared later told me that in that moment as he saw Aaron rush to gather his belongings and meet his father in the church parking lot so he could get down to the hospital, he saw faith rise up in Aaron like he had never seen before.

As all this was unfolding, Pastor Brent Parsley, head of our junior high ministry, was wrapping up the service and getting ready to dismiss the kids for the day. Pastor Jared informed him about what was happening in a hospital several miles away, and Pastor Brent said, "Before we all go, let's pray for this little girl."

Hundreds of students shifted their stance to face toward the downtown hospital, they lifted their hands and their energy and their attention toward a fragile nineteen-month-old who was fighting for her life, and they prayed. "Jesus, please do a miracle in her body," they asked. "Please heal her completely, even as we pray."

As Aaron and his father made their way to the hospital, Aaron was so full of faith that he just *knew* a miracle was about to unfold.

The tiny toddler had arrived at the hospital around 8:45 that morning, unresponsive and manifesting little brain activity. Her body was virtually destroyed. The students in our junior high group prayed at 9:07, according to Pastor Brent, who happened to catch sight of a giant digital clock in the back of the room as he bowed his head to lead the prayer. It would later be recorded by the doctor on call that sometime between 9:05 and 9:10 that morning, the little girl suddenly became responsive. Her bodily functions inexplicably had returned.

When Aaron arrived at the hospital, he gave the family hugs and offered to pray over their child. Having no idea that God was already busily working a miracle, Aaron prayed, "Lord, I know you have the power to heal this little girl. I know that you are the God of miracles and the God of life."

Just then the child's eyes popped wide open, and she said, "Mommy! Ouch!"

In Aaron's words, "We all watched a little girl who was virtually dead miraculously come back to life."

It's one thing to talk in theory about how to move through the shadowy valleys of life, but another thing altogether to put into practice our faith. To this day, the doctor and other medical staff who treated that little girl have no clue how she survived. The odds, admittedly, were against her. And her body wasn't fully developed enough to fight off brokenness like that in its own strength.

But I know how she made it. I know why she is thriving still today. And so does every other member of New Life Church. In the same time period that God allowed the Works girls to die, he chose to miraculously raise up a third. He was reminding us all that the same one who overcame death on the cross had overcome the death that we face. "In this world you will have trouble," Jesus says in John 16:33. "But take heart! I have overcome the world."

That's the end of the Grand Story, and it's a good one, isn't it? Jesus has won, and therefore we too can win. In the midst of very real death that surrounds us on every side, of relationships and bank accounts and dreams and flesh-and-blood lives, we can choose to live as victorious lovers of God instead of being known as valley dwellers who never quite emerge from the dark. We can keep our hand firmly in the grip of our Good Shepherd, knowing that because of the infusion of power we find there, there is nothing we can't overcome.

PART 2

LESSONS LEARNED
IN A CRISIS

I have known the pain of crushing circumstances

and the elation of very good days.

But through the suffering as well as the joy,

I can see how it all has matured me in Christ.

I can look back on the journey thus far and see reflected

in every step that this place is not my home,

that heaven has come, but not fully yet.

And from the victories God has given me,

I can gain strength to keep fighting a very worthy fight.

CHAPTER 4

Every Sunday
Needs a Wednesday

Hope begins in the dark,
the stubborn hope that if you just show up
and try to do the right thing, the dawn will come.
You wait and watch and work: You don't give up.
— *Anne Lamott*

IT WAS ON A SUNDAY THAT THE SENSE OF STABILITY AND PEACE WE were coming to enjoy was all but stolen from New Life Church. Bullets were fired, blood was spilled, and in a handful of minutes, what was known became unpredictable once more.

That was Sunday — Sunday, bloody Sunday.

Sunday wouldn't define us, though, because three days later Wednesday arrived. And although I didn't know it at the time, Wednesday would be our church's opportunity to say to ourselves, our God, and anyone else who happened to be listening that we refused to be defined by tragedy and that hope was still ours to claim.

Yes, Sunday happened. But a better day soon would dawn. Death and destruction would threaten us, but in the end they wouldn't have their way. Like any family that faces unthinkable tragedy, our church would gather together, grieve together, and then get busy reassuring each other that a brighter future lay ahead. And we would do so on a Wednesday — Wednesday, December 12.

That Wednesday morning, I headed into the office feeling even sicker than I had the night before. Somewhere in the early part of the week, I had picked up the unmistakable signs of the flu: body aches, a fever mixed with chills, zero appetite, and the general sense of lethargy that tells you you'd be far better off in bed.

I was also emotionally drained. I'd spent much of the previous evening at Focus on the Family's headquarters a few miles from our campus, where I camped out in their studios for several hours to conduct interviews — some live, some taped — with Larry King, Greta Van Susteren, the folks from *Good Morning America*, and others. I think it was during my chat with Larry King that I experienced a coughing spell every fifteen seconds, almost on the dot. Typically, I could space the attacks so I was coughing while Larry was talking, but on one occasion the camera cut back to me sooner than I expected and caught me downing a cupful of soda in an attempt to moisten my throat. Friends from Texas harassed me via text: "Can't you wait until the interview is over to enjoy your little snack?"

It was comic relief I needed, on a day when everything seemed empty and dark.

Earlier in the afternoon that Tuesday, I had met with New Life's overseers and executive staff. I coveted their input on immediate steps we as leaders needed to take. What was the true impact our church was facing as a result of the shooting? How should we care for members of our congregation who had seen and heard violent things? What requests did we need to make of God to endure such a difficult week? Together we dissected questions like these, in hopes of working our way toward helpful solutions.

After several hours of dialogue and heartfelt prayer, a common theme emerged: a week's time was far too long to wait before we brought the New Life family together again. We didn't want to wait until the following Sunday to hug them, to encourage them, to remind them that despite a vicious attack, we *would* get our legs under us again.

It was suggested that we hold a family meeting the following night —Wednesday night—and that we call everyone in the church to be there. After all, two family members had died. And when a loss like that happens in a natural family, the surviving members don't say to each other, "Okay, then, I guess I'll just see you at the funeral." Far from it. Typically, loved ones board the next flight or hop in their car and make their way to a common location so they can simply be together. There might not be many words exchanged during those first few hours or days, but great comfort is passed from person to person as each one's presence is felt.

Similarly, I wanted every member of New Life's congregation to have tangible proof—and soon—that we were in this valley together. And that someday we would get out. But what should our church's family meeting look like? Those of us responsible for planning it had no idea what to expect.

Back in my office that Wednesday morning, I sat back in my chair and realized that although I would be standing on a platform to address a grieving congregation in ten hours' time, I had absolutely nothing to say. "I'm spent, God," I admitted. "It's one of the most important nights in the life of our church, and for the first time in my ministry career, I have no clue what to say."

By God's great grace, I sensed a divine reply: *It's okay*, he seemed to say. *I do.* I didn't have a message to convey, but evidently my Father in heaven did. *I've even taken the liberty to write it down for you*, God continued. *Just focus on reading my Word.*

In the end I would do just that. I would stand before the people of New Life that evening and rest fully on the promises of God. Sometimes Scripture has to speak for us, and we're asked only to receive. Wednesday night was one of those times, and what a perfect gift God's Word was.

The family meeting was to begin at seven o'clock, and around six,

I watched from my office windows as cars streamed into the various parking lots surrounding our building. Suddenly a wave of compassion swelled within me. "This is a safe place to come," I thought. "I'm so glad you all are here."

We had beefed up our security presence for the meeting so that not only would our people be safe, but also they would *feel* safe. Several ill-intentioned bloggers had threatened to "come finish the work that Matthew Murray had started," and the last thing we needed was for any of those rogue plans to pan out. My team and I chose to take action to make New Life Church the safest place in all of Colorado Springs on that particular evening. To our relief, it was.

There had been a frenzy of activity during the previous twenty-four hours, as news outlets and congregation members were alerted about our gathering. Thankfully, I had been shielded from that logistical onslaught by Rob Brendle, our associate pastor at the time. He fielded every media call, coordinated plans for each local and state official who would be joining us for our meeting, and faithfully updated me every hour or so regarding the progress being made. Even on short notice, thousands were planning to show up, congregation members and dignitaries alike. Our state's governor was out of the country, but Lieutenant Governor Barbara O'Brien would be attending in his stead. Senator Wayne Allard was in session in Washington, D.C., at the time but sent a video greeting to be included in the service. Colorado's attorney general John Suthers came, as did Colorado Springs' mayor Lionel Rivera, a man who found his way to my side immediately after the shooting and stayed there until well into that first night. "You know, I have been meaning to call and introduce myself," I explained to him when he arrived on the scene on December 9. "I didn't mean for our first meeting to occur on a Sunday afternoon in a mobile police command center, but here we are."

At the family meeting, as I entered New Life's sanctuary — the Living Room, as we call it — a little before seven, I immediately noted what an interesting collision of cultures had convened. Invited guests from the city and state — elected officials, members of the Colorado Springs police force and fire department, leaders and members from other local churches — many of whom never had been inside our building, sat somewhat austerely in coats and ties, while surrounding them on all sides were six thousand radical New Lifers who were chomping at the bit to worship God. I hoped that our new friends would sense the presence of God and that they would detect an unmistakable resolve in New Life's people to see evil used for good in our church's life.

I headed down a side aisle to get to my seat but was stopped every eight or ten steps by one guest or another. I greeted all the officials and thanked them sincerely for joining us. I hugged members of our congregation and briefly prayed with ones who requested it. By the time I reached the front row, I was more than ready for the song set to start. This was the reason we'd *really* come, to exalt our great and mighty God.

Against a backdrop of poinsettias blanketing the tiered stage, and Christmas decor from the previous weekend's *Wonderland* performances, Ross Parsley took the platform and opened the family meeting by reading Psalm 42:3, 5–11:

> My tears have been my food
>   day and night,
> while men say to me all day long,
>   "Where is your God?" ...
>
> Why are you downcast, O my soul?
>   Why so disturbed within me?
> Put your hope in God,
>   for I will yet praise him,
>   my Savior and my God.
>
> My soul is downcast within me;
>   therefore I will remember you

from the land of the Jordan,
the heights of Hermon — from Mount Mizar.
Deep calls to deep
in the roar of your waterfalls;
all your waves and breakers
have swept over me.

By day the LORD directs his love,
at night his song is with me —
a prayer to the God of my life.

I say to God my Rock,
"Why have you forgotten me?
Why must I go about mourning,
oppressed by the enemy?"
My bones suffer mortal agony
as my foes taunt me,
saying to me all day long,
"Where is your God?"

Why are you downcast, O my soul?
Why so disturbed within me?
Put your hope in God,
for I will yet praise him,
my Savior and my God.

When Ross got to that last line, the congregation couldn't help but erupt in applause. It was an act of holy defiance on our part, a collective agreement that despite everything that had happened three days prior, we *still* would praise our God.

"Here's the first thing we're going to do tonight," Ross continued. "We're going to lift up our voices, and we're going to worship the God of our faith. We're going to worship the God who loves us, the God we joyfully serve. We're going to worship the Savior who rescued us from sin and death, the one who has conquered even the grave."

As we began to sing—to cry out to God in melodies and harmonies—I knew that something special was unfolding in our midst. New Life is made up of people who stay standing until you force them to sit down, who leave hands and arms outstretched toward God in worship until the last downbeat is heard, who wear a determined look on their faces despite the tears that fill their eyes. When Ross and the other worship leaders—Jared Anderson, Jon Egan, and Glenn Packiam— began the final chorus of Chris Tomlin's "How Great Is Our God," New Lifers burst into spontaneous shouts of praise and applause. As they did, I caught sight of several of the dignitaries seated to my right. I had no idea what their individual church backgrounds included, but a majority of them seemed to have a look on their faces that said, "What in the world is happening here?"

My guess was that they were trying to wrap their minds around what had become a celebration of God and of life, rather than a mournful and despondent experience. In fact, a few months later I would have my hunch confirmed by the chief of police for Colorado Springs, Richard Myers. He and I met for lunch one day, and it was the first opportunity I'd had to ask him what he thought of that Wednesday night gathering. He is a follower of Jesus Christ, but even so, he admitted that the energetic worship caught him a little off guard. "That was my first time in a ... charismatic ... church—is that what you call it? And it was *way* out of my comfort zone."

Regardless of how comfortable or uncomfortable our guests may have been at the family meeting, one thing is sure: Chief Myers and the others could see it written on countless New Lifers' faces, and could sense it in every outstretched arm, that as a church we were not going to resign ourselves to a spirit of fear, but rather to the spirit of power, love, and a sound mind, courtesy of a heavenly Father who right then and there was making good on his promise never to leave us or forsake us. I said as much in seven simple words as I took the platform that night.

I told the congregation that what was happening that night was pleasing to God in heaven, because what we were doing was making a declaration, early and firm: "We will not be governed by fear," I said to those gathered in the Living Room. "We will *not* be governed by fear" —they were words that had been born nearly thirty years prior, when I had found that rope around my neck thanks to a bunch of foolish high school boys. As I stood on that stage at New Life, I wanted to say, "We will not be bullied," but nobody would have understood what lay behind my words. Still, it was the truth. Because of a single painful event I had known as a kid, I refused to be bullied again. In my spirit as I stood before my congregation, I was saying, "I am not going to let a human being who is being used as a pawn in Satan's hand frighten, intimidate, or bully me. And tonight you must resolve that you won't either."

I knew that we as a body had been attacked. I knew that we had our work cut out for us in terms of convincing people that New Life was a safe place to be. I knew that for some, it would take weeks or months or even years to move past the troubling images they saw on Sunday, December 9. But I also knew that God's Word remains true, regardless of whatever else transpires. And it is his Word that promises that we as believers are kept in the palm of his hand, where *nothing* can snatch us away: not Satan, not his minions, not the Matthew Murrays of the world. Nothing can remove us from the place where God says we live. Our lives are governed by the great God of our faith; we must not be governed by fear.

As I spoke those words over the crowd that night, the people applauded passionately in response. Frankly, I wanted to applaud too. God was doing great things in us. He was doing great things in *me*. I'm a pretty confident person these days, someone who really does refuse to live in a perpetual state of fear and insecurity, but things weren't always that way. Over the years, I have done my fair share of wrestling to get free from timidity's grip, knowing that God's eyes really are on me and that my life does in fact matter to him. An insecure, fear-stricken person can't accept those truths. Instead, he has bought the lie that God is ignoring him, that the King of the universe must have far too much on his plate to trouble himself with a meaningless peon like him. There certainly were times in my own life when I could relate to that.

When Pam and I moved from Hereford to Southlake, Texas, so I could accept the ministry role at Gateway Church, I was tempted to feel inferior to some of the people we met. I had grown up poor: the five members of my family lived in an eight-hundred-square-foot house my mom and dad built by hand, my father was a blue-collar factory worker who survived one paycheck at a time, and I remember money always being tight. Many people in the Dallas – Fort Worth area couldn't relate. They grew up in situations where there was enough money to fund not only new clothes and meals in nice restaurants but also annual vacations, college educations, and a car for each member of the family.

For three or four years leading up to my transition to New Life, it was as if the Holy Spirit stuck a bull's-eye on my forehead and took dead aim at me anytime I caved to insecure thoughts. Those memories of being bullied as a kid or of growing up in a family that consistently had too much month left at the end of its money would creep into my consciousness, and immediately God would prod me toward his Word.

The passage he most frequently brought to mind comes from 1 Peter 2, which says of Jesus, "When they hurled their insults at him, he did not retaliate; when he suffered, he made no threats. Instead, he entrusted himself to him who judges justly. He himself bore our sins in his body on the tree, so that we might die to sins and live for righteousness; by his wounds you have been healed. For you were like sheep going astray, but now you have returned to the Shepherd and Overseer of your souls" (vv. 23 – 25).

The one who had been hurling insults at me was Satan himself. As I eyed other people's vast properties, sprawling homes, fancy cars, elaborate wardrobes, and expensive vacations, the accuser of my soul would taunt me with statements such as, "You'll never be able to afford that. And you'll never fit in with those who do."

During those days, God asked me to dig down deep and explore what really was causing my insecure feelings. I had been a believer in him for years by then, but did I truly believe I was safe in his grip?

I'm not sure how many rounds I went in my fight against insecurity, but by the time I called Colorado Springs home, by God's grace I had won. God had taught me privately what I needed to know so that once the hot lights of public scrutiny were threatening to blind me on the heels of horrific tragedy, I could stand confidently on that which was true. And what was true on that Wednesday night remains steadfastly true today: the only way you and I endure the valley of death is by claiming God-given courage as our own. We really can entrust ourselves — our lives, our safety, our future — to the one who judges justly, the loving Overseer of our souls.

From the platform during our family meeting, I looked into the eyes of men, women, and kids who were just as determined as I was to move through the valley we were in. We weren't going to pitch our tent there; instead, we would place one foot in front of another and slowly but surely get out.

After the great Old Testament leader Moses died, his aide Joshua was tapped by God to take the reins and lead the Israelites across the Jordan River. And as God commissioned Joshua for this new role, he told him not once, not twice, but three times to be strong and courageous. "Be strong and courageous," he says in Joshua 1:6. "Be strong and *very* courageous," he says one verse later (emphasis added). And then, in case Joshua missed the first two installments, verse 9 reads this way: "Have I not commanded you? Be strong and courageous. Do not be terrified; do not be discouraged, for the LORD your God will be with you wherever you go."

From the tenor in the room that Wednesday night, I could tell that the people of New Life knew what I firmly believed to be true: this was our Joshua moment. Sunday had threatened to rob us of our peace, our solidarity, and our faith. But on Wednesday night we would say no.

On Wednesday we would choose to claim not fear but courage —to live, to love, to *engage.*

At any given time, courage is either entering into you or departing from you. It's always doing one or the other; it is not static. When you're *dis*couraged—when courage drips its way out of you like water from a leaky hose—nothing you do seems worthwhile. Every molehill shows up as a mountain, and every dilemma is a debilitating crisis just waiting to take you down. Everything negative in life is amplified, and whatever good exists fades to gray.

But when you're *en*couraged—when courage is coming *in*—you feel as if you can do just about anything in God's name and will experience a fair measure of success. You charge hell with a water pistol and serve like your hair is on fire, not knowing what else to do with your massive influx of holy audacity.

I think one of the old standbys in Satan's arsenal is the strategy of discouragement. John 10:10 tells us that he exists only to steal, kill, and destroy. And when I trace back his most effective ploys in my life, I find that every single snare I've gotten myself tangled up in began with a mere hint of discouragement.

"This job isn't panning out like I'd hoped ..."

"My marriage isn't as easy as I thought it would be ..."

"Surely, God knows I need more money than this to survive ..."

Thoughts like those seem so subtle, until you check back a month or a year later and realize you're living hip-deep in destructive ways. I couldn't bear the thought of that happening to the church I was growing to love, but unless we reversed some errant thinking, that's exactly what would unfold.

"This church is done ..."

"We must be living under a curse ..."

"We'll never recover from this ..."

"Our best days are obviously long gone ..."

Because one young man with a gun made one choice on one otherwise average Sunday morning, many among our body of believers were left to fight discouragement's ploys. Would we cave to Satan's schemes and hand over our peace and joy? Or would we persevere in the wake of an unthinkably tough time and tell the world that our God still reigns?

With these thoughts in mind, I asked the entire congregation to join hands as I prayed for perseverance to have its way. "I want you to receive courage from one another," I told the crowd. "I want you to receive strength from one another. I want you to receive *hope* from one another, as you hold each other's hands."

Looking out on the unbroken cord of prayerful men, women, and children, I thanked God for being our steady source of strength. I thanked him for his Son, Jesus, who came to earth from heaven, who lived a sinless life, who was willing to be crucified, and who — on the third day following that gruesome death — triumphantly overcame the world. I expressed our shared gratitude to God for the power of his presence, a presence that banishes *all* forms of fear. And I asked him, by his grace, to keep our hearts and minds according to Christ Jesus' will.

As people found their seats and the room quieted once more, I explained to the crowd the facts of what had taken place on December 9. As agonizing as it was to lay out those events once more, nothing was harder for me than confirming the loss of Stephanie and Rachel Works. I am a parent. And as every parent knows, there is nothing worse than the prospect of outliving your kids. To know that not only had Marie and David Works lost two of their girls, but also they had lost them to a bloody, murderous rage, was more sobering than I could adequately convey with words.

"Tonight, we want to pray for David Works, the father of the two precious young girls who were killed," I said. "He is still in the hospital, recovering from surgery, and he needs our heartfelt prayers.

"The Works family was in our east parking lot on Sunday," I continued, "and they were leaving church late for a reason. They had stuck around to talk with people, to minister to people, to serve the body of Christ. That's what New Lifers do. And that's what the Workses had done. They loved on people and then walked out to their van to load up and head to lunch. And then David and two of his girls were shot.

"As you know by now, Stephanie and Rachel Works were the victims of Sunday's attack...."

As soon as the sentence came out of my mouth, my throat all but closed up. I must have stood there, silent, for twenty full seconds, trying desperately to compose myself, trying somehow to find words to go on. I thought about Marie and David's loss. I thought about Matthew Murray's parents' loss. I thought about the families of the kids in Arvada who had been shot and killed by the very same gun. And the dad in me wanted to weep.

Theological positions on life and death do little to soothe the raw nerves when tragedy hits close to home. If you've ever been at the bedside of an intimate follower of Christ who is about to die, then you know it's a completely different experience than sitting by the deathbed of someone who has been living far from God. Believers recognize that they are sojourners on the earth, that they are pilgrims passing through this place, en route to an eternal home.

Still, the Works girls were only eighteen and sixteen years old, with bright futures they were determined to pursue. As young teenagers, they had given their lives to ministry and had recently returned from a mission trip to China. They already knew at their tender ages that the joy you get from serving Christ is like no other joy around. These girls weren't casual followers of Jesus. They were devoted in their walk. And while I knew they were rejoicing in heaven that Wednesday night, I *still* found it tough to move on.

Eventually, during my period of choked-up silence, applause in honor of the Works girls began to swell from every section of our church. The courage I'd asked God to give those worshipers they now were returning to me.

As a body, we prayed a prayer of comfort for those who had been hurt. We told God that because we have received mercy, we offer mercy to those who need it. Because we have received forgiveness, we offer forgiveness. And because we have received love, we offer deep love in response. "We give back all of the things that we have received from you in heaven," I said on our congregation's behalf, once I was finally able to speak. "And tonight we choose to release any judgment, any offense, any hurt, any fear. In Jesus' name, we let go of those things now."

We thanked God for the evident fruit that had been present in Stephanie's and Rachel's lives, and we praised him that because of their faith, they were worshiping at Jesus' side then and there.

As God had promised, some specific passages of Scripture had been laid on my heart as I considered what to share that night. The first was Psalm 27:1–6, which reads,

> The LORD is my light and my salvation—
>   whom shall I fear?
> The LORD is the stronghold of my life—
>   of whom shall I be afraid?
> When evil men advance against me
>   to devour my flesh,
> when my enemies and my foes attack me,
>   they will stumble and fall.
> Though an army besiege me,
>   my heart will not fear;
> though war break out against me,
>   even then will I be confident.
>
> One thing I ask of the LORD,
>   this is what I seek:

that I may dwell in the house of the LORD
    all the days of my life,
to gaze upon the beauty of the LORD
    and to seek him in his temple.
For in the day of trouble
    he will keep me safe in his dwelling;
he will hide me in the shelter of his tabernacle
    and set me high upon a rock.
Then my head will be exalted
    above the enemies who surround me;
at his tabernacle will I sacrifice with shouts of joy;
    I will sing and make music to the LORD.

How desperately we needed that reassurance Wednesday night, that we can be confident amid the war that rages around us, that in this day of trouble, we are *always* safe in God's dwelling. As I came to the psalmist David's closing thought, I looked into the faces of an expectant congregation and said, "Let me tell you what will happen this Sunday at New Life Church. We will have church services at nine a.m. and at eleven a.m., and we will *sing and make music to the Lord.*"

The people of New Life cheered as I continued to read from the Psalms. "Psalm 46 says this: 'God is our refuge and strength, an ever-present help in trouble. Therefore we will not fear, though the earth give way and the mountains fall into the heart of the sea, though its waters roar and foam and the mountains quake with their surging'" (vv. 1–3).

I could sense our collective belief rising as I continued to read that God was still our refuge. "'There is a river whose streams make glad the city of God,'" I said, quoting verses 4 through 7 of that psalm, "'the holy place where the Most High dwells. God is within her, she will not fall; God will help her at break of day. Nations are in uproar, kingdoms fall; he lifts his voice, the earth melts. The LORD Almighty is with us; the God of Jacob is our fortress.'"

As is always the case, the simple act of reading God's Word and then claiming it as truth to live by did not return void. What began to unfold all around us was a spirit of optimism, of hope, of resolve. I asked Ross, the other worship leaders, and the choir to take the stage once more and told New Life that I could think of no better way to close our time together than to do what we do best. "We are going to end by worshiping our God together," I said. "By the words of our testimony, we will declare to a watching world that God's power and presence are *real*."

The crowd clapped and cheered over the opportunity to praise our heavenly Father, but none of us could have anticipated the time of worship that was to come.

Days after Pastor Ted Haggard left New Life Church, members of the congregation began meeting at the church to pray, both early every morning and late into the night most every night of the week. The scandal had rattled many of them to their core, and their goal during those times together was simply to seek God's wisdom regarding how to move forward in faith.

Our youth group had also been rattled, prompting David Perkins, one of our youth pastors, to teach at that month's youth retreat on the subject of being "overcomers." After David's talk, worship leader Jon Egan read from the book of Revelation the account of Satan—there called the "accuser of our brothers"—being hurled down from heaven to the earth, him and his angels with him.

> Then I heard a loud voice in heaven say:
>> "Now have come the salvation and the power and
>>> the kingdom of our God,
>>> and the authority of his Christ.
>> For the accuser of our brothers,

who accuses them before our God day and night,
    has been hurled down.
They overcame him
    by the blood of the Lamb
    and by the word of their testimony;
they did not love their lives so much
    as to shrink from death.
Therefore rejoice, you heavens
    and you who dwell in them!
But woe to the earth and the sea,
    because the devil has gone down to you!
He is filled with fury,
    because he knows that his time is short."

—*Revelation 12:10–12*

As Jon passionately read that passage to the young people gathered at the meeting that night, he instinctively began strumming his guitar to the cadence of the words. The idea that Satan and his evil schemes could be overtaken by Jesus' blood and by the powerful testimonies of those who call him Lord gripped Jon, and within minutes a new song was born. "We will overcome!" Jon shouted against the strains of his guitar. "We will overcome, by the blood of the Lamb and the word of our testimony! *Everyone*, overcome."

Prophetically, Jon was singing the very Scripture that our church would cling to thirteen months later. At the close of that significant Wednesday night family meeting, "Overcome" is what we sang.

For more than a year we had sung that song, but that night it became our anthem. As soon as the opening guitar riffs reverberated throughout the auditorium, the congregation reflexively and passionately applauded. Ross Parsley and Jon led us as we sang:

Seated above, enthroned in the Father's love
Destined to die, poured out for all mankind

God's only Son, perfect and spotless One
He never sinned, but suffered as if he did
All authority, every victory is Yours
All authority, every victory is Yours
Savior, worthy of honor and glory, worthy of all our praise,
For You overcame
Jesus, awesome in power forever, awesome and great is Your
     name
For You overcame
Power in hand, seeking the Father's plan
Sending us out, light in this broken land
All authority, every victory is Yours
All authority, every victory is Yours!
Savior, worthy of honor and glory, worthy of all our praise,
For You overcame
Jesus, awesome in power forever, awesome and great is Your
     name
For You overcame

By the time we reached the bridge of the song, I thought the entire place might explode in waves of praise to the God we love and serve. "We will overcome, by the blood of the Lamb and the word of our testimony," we sang. "Everyone, overcome."

Despite his best efforts, Ross Parsley at one point was too choked up to sing. I knew how he felt: six thousand people weren't just singing. We were proclaiming a new posture as a church. Regardless of what had happened, we were *determined* that through God we would indeed overcome.

I'm not sure of the intended length of Jon's original song, but that night we sang it for nearly ten minutes straight. Nobody wanted it to end. And as I returned to the platform to dismiss the service, I felt supernaturally uplifted. I knew I wasn't alone. I told the congregation that there was one more thing we needed to do before we headed home for the night. I invited those who needed grief counseling and ministry to head to various parts of the building where those services would be provided, and then I asked everyone else to walk every square inch of the campus and anoint the entire place with oil. I received blank stares at first, which I later discovered was because native Louisianans tend to say "awl" when they really mean "oil."

"If you brought anointing *oil*," I carefully enunciated, "then I would ask that you please scatter throughout all of our buildings—head into children's classrooms, high school rooms, the foyer, the coffee shop, the prayer chapel—and rededicate this place for God's purposes."

The first sight I'd had of the building the morning after the shooting was marked by blood and carnage. But on Wednesday night we had an opportunity to reclaim its beauty and peacefulness. Certainly, the building itself is not holy, but it *is* special. It's the place where we as a local body of believers gather week in and week out to worship God, and while the walls and beams and hallways are not sacred, the wonderful memories made there are.

God had given us that property, that building, and the mission we were pursuing. None of us wanted to surrender even one inch of all that to the Evil One. Satan had tried to steal the peace we prized, and now we could visibly symbolize that he had failed.

There's a great scene from the epic movie *Saving Private Ryan*, in which the German army has pinned down the Allied forces on the beaches of France, and the Allied soldiers are all forced to hide behind anything that might offer protection from the barrage of artillery fire. On every side, men are being blown to pieces by machine gun sprays, when the character played by Tom Hanks yells, "We cannot stay here! We must get off this beach—we are all *dead* men if we stay here!"

It must have seemed like an odd thing to say, given that the most obvious thing those soldiers thought they should do was to stay protected in their safe huddle instead of charging out into the dangerous unknown. But Hanks's character knew something his troops did not: the war is never won unless the enemy is actively engaged.

In the end, those soldiers did not stay on the beaches of Normandy. With great courage and in many cases tremendous sacrifice, they forged ahead and liberated France from the tyranny of the Nazi regime. And as I watched the courageous men and women of New Life Church pray inside various classrooms and anoint doorposts in our facility with oil late that Wednesday night, I realized that we too were getting off the beach. We were sad. We were grieving. We had mourning left to do. But we still were a people of faith. And faith always brings hope, faith always brings peace, faith *always* brings the healing we need.

If you are in that same spot now—you're sad, you're grieving, there is mourning over some loss still left to do—please know that what was true for us as a church is true for you today. Climbing out of the valley is never easy, but better days really do lie ahead.

CHAPTER 5

Disney Doesn't Do Christianity

Dependence, humility, simplicity, cooperation, abandon —
these are qualities greatly prized in the spiritual life,
but extremely elusive for people who live in comfort.
— Philip Yancey

THREE WEEKS BEFORE THE SHOOTING OCCURRED, MY FAMILY AND I boarded a jet bound for Disneyland. Thanksgiving was approaching, and Pam and I decided it would be a perfect time to enjoy a family vacation before the busyness that always surrounds Christmastime kicked in.

From the moment we passed through Disney's colorful entrance gates in Anaheim, California, until the end of our last day there, I was reminded of how appealing perfection can be. If it's not the mission statement of Disneyland, it ought to be: "Always perfect, all the time."

At Disneyland, everyone is always smiling, shows are always entertaining, and despite millions of messy visitors tromping through the park each and every year, there is never a speck of trash to be found lying on the ground. At Disneyland, nothing is dark, nothing is dreary, and nothing deflates your day. Instead, because of the ridiculously cheery surroundings, even as a grown-up who has a family, a mortgage, and a "real people" job, I couldn't help but laugh and sing along with the It's a Small World figurines, who cock their heads back and forth in cadence with the memorable (and annoying) song.

For kids, the situation seems even *better* than perfect, since everything they could possibly want is not only available but also positioned at their eye level. Cotton candy, soft drinks, their very own pair of Mickey Mouse ears — watching Abram and Callie rush up to kiosk after kiosk and then turn toward Pam and me with pleading "Can we get one?" looks on their faces helped us better understand how the Disney fortune has been made. It's "the happiest place on earth," their slogan proudly states. And although this makes for a fantastic vacation philosophy, it's hardly the basis for a sound theological framework.

Less than one month after our perfect visit to always-perfect-all-the-time Disneyland, I found myself holed up in my church office with a gunman firing shots one floor below. In the time it took for Matthew Murray to start shooting, the life of our church had become a stage on which the words from John 14 – 16 were unexpectedly and unfortunately played out. In those three chapters of the Bible, vast quantities of red ink are used to spell out all of Jesus' promises about how we would face heartaches and trials in this world, about how we would know suffering beyond what we could ever imagine.

He looks into his disciples' eyes and prepares them for tough days ahead. He speaks to them not about their health and wealth and happiness but about the persecution that will be theirs someday. He talks to them in metaphor, reminding them that they won't be left as orphans, that they are branches that must stay connected to the vine, that they will know suffering on par with the pain of childbirth, but that someday they'll remember that anguish no more. Then he closes his comments with a key reminder that despite the demoralizing facts he has just laid out, they still should take heart, because their Savior has victoriously overcome the world. Those disciples were going to see some difficult things, but they would one day overcome. It was a helpful reminder to me on December 9, that even in the midst of terrible suffering unfolding around me, one day I'd be all right again too.

I had read those chapters in the book of John on several occasions before. But prior to my coming to New Life, they had remained theoretical at best. I hadn't really had to face persecution when I was a pastor in Dallas – Fort Worth. From time to time people in the congregation would get mad at me or would make accusations about me, but I had never been a target of violence. I had never had my life threatened in any way. Gateway was a prosperous church with resources to spare, and we were growing at a rapid rate; the last thing on my mind was being persecuted for my faith.

But since December 9, I have read those verses in an altogether different way. I now cling to those promises Christ made about never leaving or forsaking us, about not abandoning us as orphans when we're in pain. They are far more than mere theory to me today; they are the spiritual oxygen I breathe. If my theology must make room for suffering, then I want to know that when those trials close in on me, my loving God is also near.

In Matthew 16:24, Jesus says that anyone who comes after him must be willing to deny himself, take up his cross, and follow him. The cross is a symbol of death — *horrific* death. What he was saying is that true followership means being willing to die each day, and to die an undignified death, if we are asked to do so.

I believe this is why so many of Christ's disciples along the way simply got up and left Jesus' side. They couldn't bear the thought of having to sacrifice their agendas, their priorities, their habits, their passions, their very *lives* — all for the sake of God.

It's also why so many pastors today won't preach the message of promised suffering. If they themselves aren't willing to take up their crosses, how on earth can they compel others to follow suit? The net effect is a generation of believers in God who have bought into the Christian experience that Disney would produce, if Disney did Christianity.

I recently came across a book by Jonathan Acuff entitled *Stuff Christians Like*, and one of the chapters offers a humorous look at what it must be like to work at a church:

> Don't you wish you worked at a church? That would be such a dream job! I've never been blessed that way, but my assumption is that, other than on Sunday, a church job is kind of like having a really long quiet time. You probably get to read the Bible all day and take long breaks in your prayer closet and spend eight hours a day growing your own spiritual life.
>
> I'm sure the phone rings sometimes, like when someone needs a casserole of hope after a death in the family or a youth group van breaks down, but for the most part, I imagine the average day is filled with a lot of "me time."
>
> And God is your boss. How cool is that? There's no politics or in-fighting or gossip like at the average corporate job. It's just a collection of people, a family really, living out of the gifts God has given them. Loving on each other. Everyone is all on the same page, pouring out to each other the love that God is pouring into them. Don't you want to hug this book right now, just thinking about that?[1]

I should mention here that the page facing this particular quote in Acuff's book boasts a drawing of this "ideal" church, comprising a quaint building with a tall steeple on top, a rainbow and butterflies hovering overhead, and cheery unicorns prancing through a field of daisies out front. And as I looked over the drawing, I was reminded of how many Christians really do expect church to work that way. What's more, they expect *life* to work like that. They anticipate cotton candy and unicorns and Mickey Mouse ears and are utterly shocked when suffering shows up instead. But as I mentioned earlier, suffering is what we were promised, both by Jesus and by the apostle Paul. In fact, much of the New Testament was written from a dank, dark prison cell where Paul was being held captive because of his faith in Jesus Christ — not from some idealized dreamland where all is blissful and bright.

In 2 Corinthians 11, Paul recounts the sufferings he had known for the sake of Christ:

> I've worked much harder, been jailed more often, beaten up more times than I can count, and at death's door time after time. I've been flogged five times with the Jews' thirty-nine lashes, beaten by Roman rods three times, pummeled with rocks once. I've been shipwrecked three times, and immersed in the open sea for a night and a day. In hard traveling year in and year out, I've had to ford rivers, fend off robbers, struggle with friends, struggle with foes. I've been at risk in the city, at risk in the country, endangered by desert sun and sea storm, and betrayed by those I thought were my brothers. I've known drudgery and hard labor, many a long and lonely night without sleep, many a missed meal, blasted by the cold, naked to the weather.
>
> — *2 Corinthians 11:23–27 MSG*

Yet three books after Paul's litany of affliction — in Philippians 4 — we read these words, also from the mouth of Paul:

> I have learned to be content whatever the circumstances. I know what it is to be in need, and I know what it is to have plenty. I have learned the secret of being content in any and every situation, whether well fed or hungry, whether living in plenty or in want. I can do everything through him who gives me strength.
>
> — *Philippians 4:11–13*

Regardless of what happened *to* Paul, what was happening *in* him continued steady and sure. If his circumstances caused him to die, then he would quickly find himself at the side of his Lord. If his circumstances allowed him to live, then he would keep fighting for the cause of Christ, clinging to the hope that was his in Christ Jesus. Either way, he won. Either way, he prevailed. Either way, he could choose to be content, because *God* would provide his strength.

Suffice it to say, it's a far cry from much of what is being taught in many churches today.

Many of today's preaching trends—such as the expectation that with God leading the way, we'll always be happy, all the time—date back at least half a century. In the 1950s, after the Second World War had come and gone and the country was finally experiencing some degree of prosperity, pastors stepped onto stages all across the United States and said, "God's favor is on this country because of what we did in World War II. Therefore we will be a people of great comfort from this point forward."

Church leaders from nearly every denomination declared that the dues had been paid and that health and wealth were now the name of the game. It was a dangerous premise to hold to, but the heresy was so pleasing to the ears of those who had survived the Great Depression that congregations began to grow. Get saved, get rich, never get sick, and enjoy a perpetual Disneyland experience—who wouldn't want a life like that?

Admittedly, there were some positive byproducts of the teaching. God *does* want to bless his people, and the Bible *does* promise success to those who meditate on his Word day and night (Josh. 1:8). But to claim wild prosperity here on planet Earth apart from suffering of any kind is to blatantly disregard what the rest of God's Word clearly states.

Scripture shows that some believers will be brought before judges on Christ's account. Some will be imprisoned for their faith, just as Paul was. Some will be persecuted for the sake of God's name. Some will be put to death. As we saw earlier, when it comes to hardships in this life, it's not a matter of *if*; it's a matter of when. We know *precisely* what we've been promised. The only question that remains, then, is *why?*

Each week, I hear faithful followers of Christ pose that question more than any other. A dad dies of cancer, a couple buries a child, a successful businessman loses his job, a spouse ditches what seemed on the surface to be a healthy marriage, a homeowner finds a foreclosure notice in her mailbox, a gunman shows up on a church campus and randomly opens fire — these situations and scores of others unfold, and with pleading hearts we ask, "Why?"

"Why me?"

"Why us?"

"Why now?"

"Why is God allowing this suffering to happen when we've done absolutely nothing wrong?"

The answer, it turns out, is found in the first chapter of the book of James.

James 1:2–4 says, "Consider it pure joy, my brothers, whenever you face trials of many kinds, because you know that the testing of your faith develops perseverance. Perseverance must finish its work so that you may be mature and complete, not lacking anything."

Now, I don't want to argue with God about how he chose to write the Bible, but I think those three verses should have appeared in the opposite order. Nobody I know who is facing a trial immediately says, "Yes! Oh, *joy!* Another trial has come my way!"

It just doesn't happen.

But that's what the text says we should do. "Consider it pure *joy* ...," the verse reads, "whenever you face trials of many kinds" (emphasis added). And why are we to consider it pure joy? Because it is the testing of our faith that produces perseverance. But even *that* is not very good news, because most likely it means the trial is going to last for a long time. So we're supposed to cheer over the need to develop the perseverance that will help us get used to our terrible situation so we can endure it for an awful long time? Oh, joy!

But just before I fall headlong into a pit of deep depression, verse 4 shows up, thankfully: "Perseverance must finish its work so that you may be mature and complete, not lacking anything." Another translation says it like this: "Don't try to get out of anything prematurely. Let it do its work so you become mature and well-developed, not deficient in any way" (MSG).

Now you see why I think the verses are totally out of order. If God would have simply started with the question, "Do you want to be totally mature in the Christ-following life?" people like you and me could have first gotten on board with the goal before he dropped the bombshell news of how that actually gets done. "You're going to have to face hard times," he would say, "but through the process of enduring those trials, you will become complete, lacking nothing, whole in every conceivable way. Joy will be yours. Peace will be yours. Power will be yours as well. But you'll never realize these wonderful byproducts of faith until you first walk through tough situations in life."

Our theology *must* leave room for suffering, because the testing of our faith is how we grow. In other words, faith that has never been tested cannot be trusted. In fact, *nothing* that hasn't been tested should be trusted, which is why we enlist inspectors to come check out a house before we agree to purchase it. We want to know if the foundation is sound, the plumbing is reliable, the electrical system is correctly wired. We *test* these things so that once we move into that beautiful new home, we can trust them to function properly.

My faith was tested on December 9, 2007. Certainly, that wasn't the first time it has been tested, but it probably is the most significant test I've known. As a result of that experience, I trust my faith in God more than I've ever trusted it before. It's sound. It's sturdy. It will stand tall, even when circumstances come crashing down. I am more confident than ever in God's promises to be near me, to sustain me, to provide for me, and to help me persevere through tough times. But it took considering my trial a joy to get to that much-needed perspective.

So if trials and tribulation are guaranteed in this life in order to enable us to become mature followers of Jesus Christ, how do we learn to endure those situations that threaten to do us in?

In the days, weeks, months, and years following the shooting, God provided me answers to that deep question. He reminded me how to leave room in my theology for suffering and how to walk through suffering with grace and strength. The first reminder he offered was that a commitment made to Jesus Christ is *anything* but a casual commitment. When you and I say yes to following Christ, we're saying, "God, I'm going *all in*."

In the familiar story of Shadrach, Meshach, and Abednego facing the flames of a fiery furnace because they wouldn't cave to King Nebuchadnezzar's demands for them to worship foreign gods, they proved what it means to be all in. "Your threat means nothing to us," they said to the king. "If you throw us in the fire, the God we serve can rescue us from your roaring furnace and anything else you might cook up, O king. But even if he doesn't, it wouldn't make a bit of difference, O king. We still wouldn't serve your gods or worship the gold statue you set up" (Dan. 3:16–18 MSG).

We see further evidence of an all-in attitude in the first-century church of Jerusalem, as described in Acts 4:32–35. Believers were "one in heart and mind" and "shared everything they had," to the point where nobody in their midst experienced a single unmet need. They had taken the words of Jesus seriously when he said that the two greatest commandments in existence were to "love the Lord your God with all your heart and with all your soul and with all your mind" and to "love your neighbor as yourself" (Matt. 22:37, 39).

What God reminded me of after the shooting was that part of what it means to follow Christ is to make an all-in commitment before knowing what trials and challenges we will face, a commitment to follow him no matter what the cost. And to *keep* that all-in commitment once the seasons of suffering emerge.

In addition to this, God reminded me that a second way to walk well through suffering is simply to *confront the pain.*

The story is told in John 11 of Jesus losing his close friend Lazarus. Mary and Martha, Lazarus's sisters, had sent word to Jesus, telling him that Lazarus had fallen ill and was close to death, but despite being less than two miles from where Lazarus and the women were, Jesus chose to wait several days before making the short trip to see them. By that time it was too late. Lazarus was already gone.

When Jesus finally arrived in Bethany, Martha approached him and said, "Lord, if you had been here, my brother would not have died" (John 11:21). Martha's sister, Mary, had the very same words for Christ. Verse 32 says that as soon as she found Jesus, she fell to his feet and said, "Lord, if you had been here, my brother would not have died."

At this point in the story, Lazarus had been dead for four full days. He had been laid in a tomb, a large stone had been rolled in front of it, and everyone assumed he was gone. As Jesus took in the situation and saw tears rolling down Mary's cheeks, the text says, he was "deeply moved in spirit and troubled" (v. 33), a phrase that in the original Greek version means he emitted a deep or guttural *groaning.* Then Jesus wept.

Now, Jesus was well aware that mere moments later he would walk over to the tomb where Lazarus was buried, ask a couple of onlookers to move the stone away, and declare, "Lazarus, come out!" (v. 43). He had told the disciples as much just a few days before. So what was up with all the teary drama, given what was about to occur? Why didn't Jesus say, "Listen, Mary, no crying necessary here. Watch what I'm about to do"?

I believe that while Jesus ministered on planet Earth, he never passed up an opportunity to show us by his example how we are to respond to the situations we inevitably face in life. He was both fully God and fully human, and when he stopped and cried over his good friend's death, he poignantly showcased the fully human part of that equation. In his weeping and groaning, Jesus reminded us that it's okay not to be okay. In one fleeting scene in Scripture, he modeled for us how to mourn.

As human beings, you and I both have to learn to confront our pain—to acknowledge it and to grieve. Whether we're talking about the loss of a loved one or the loss of a career, a bank account, or a dream, it is critical to stop, to weep, to groan. I think of families who have experienced the sudden loss of a house, either to fire or to a flood. Sure, it was just drywall and two-by-fours, but their most precious memories were made inside. It was their first "real" purchase. It was the place where their children were raised. It was their family's haven, the spot where they would rest and relate and know peace.

Or what about people who have experienced the sudden loss of a marriage? A husband thought the union would last forever, but then one day divorce papers were served. "But she was my high school sweetheart," he laments. "She was *everything* in my life." Regardless of who is at fault in a split like that, division *always* hurts.

I think of countless New Lifers who experienced the sudden loss of their leader. One Sunday several years ago their senior pastor was teaching them the Word of God; the next Sunday he was gone.

What do you do when sudden loss occurs? I believe Jesus would say, "You mourn."

As I said, I've been part of a local church since my boyhood years, and yet I can count on one hand the number of sermons I've heard on how to grieve well. We talk a lot about the good news but neglect to mention that life sometimes turns bad. For instance, how many times have you been directed to the words of Ecclesiastes 7:3? "Sorrow is better than laughter," it says, "because a sad face is good for the heart." In our comfort-seeking society, most people would read those words and come away saying, "Huh? How can sorrow possibly be better than laughter?"

What Solomon, the writer of Ecclesiastes, knew that you and I would do well to remember is that the reason a sad face is good for the heart is that it is in our sadness that pain gets confronted, once and for all. Having pain confront us and choosing to confront that pain ourselves are two very different things. Confronting our pain means saying, "I know I've just taken a hit here, a hit that really hurt."

"Something terrible did happen."

"I am hurting as a result."

"*We* are hurting as a result."

"This is hard, but it is real."

Admitting truths such as these forces the internal protesting to cease. It invites Jesus into the situation so the process of restoration can begin. "The heart of the wise is in the house of mourning," Solomon said in Ecclesiastes 7:4. It's when we stop to truly grieve a loss that God can intervene.

The alternative, of course, is denial, in which we utterly resist what is real. We talk ourselves out of believing that something bad has just unfolded and that we were wounded as a result. This approach does nothing for our personal wholeness and keeps God's healing ways at bay.

Jewish people have a practice to help them acknowledge the reality of their pain, and it's one that I find incredibly useful. In that culture, there are five designated times each year when Jews are encouraged to mourn the loss of loved ones who died during the twelve months that have passed. Those five occasions include the four major Jewish holidays — Passover, Hanukkah, Rosh Hashanah, and Yom Kippur — and the anniversary of the loved one's death.

Think about that for a moment. Clearly, it makes sense to grieve on the anniversary of the date someone died. But to also grieve on a holiday, when celebration and excitement fill the air? The Jewish people believe it to be completely appropriate, and I happen to think they are right. This collision of emotions — joy, mourning, laughter, grief; up, down, up, down; high, low, high, low — is the rhythm of a healthy human soul. "Weeping may remain for a night," David affirmed in Psalm 30:5, "but rejoicing comes in the morning."

In other words, it's perfectly acceptable to be down one moment and up the next. It's okay to weep until your eyes are puffy and bloodshot and your head throbs with the weight of your grief — and then moments later find yourself laughing over a lighthearted aspect of life.

During funerals, you've probably seen the same dynamic I have observed over the years: At one moment in a funeral home or a church auditorium some will be weeping, others will be stone-faced, and still others will be chatting animatedly with those seated to their left or their right. Everyone is experiencing the same event, but they are processing it in a dozen different ways. What's more, some of those who were weeping are fine two weeks later, while some of the chatty ones later cry themselves to sleep every night.

The takeaway is this: although our timelines may vary, we must allow ourselves space to grieve. It may seem wise to plow through the suffering and move on to happier and more life-giving days. But in order to reflect the life Jesus lived, we must agree to confront our pain.

If there was a third reminder God offered up regarding how we at New Life could walk well through seasons of intense suffering, it was to recognize that the heavenly state we yearn for has not yet fully come.

A pastor friend of mine has spent most of her adult life counseling people through the stages of grief. One woman she worked with along the way was Jane,[2] a woman I'd met when I was at Gateway. Previously Jane had been in ministry with her husband, who was a youth pastor at the time. Everyone who knew them during that season of life thought their marriage was solid as a rock; what they couldn't possibly have guessed was that after work each day, Jane's husband would come home from the church and viciously beat his wife to a pulp.

Eventually Jane exposed her husband for the abuser he really was and created a new life for herself that was far away from him. But for many years following her narrow escape, a haunting thought plagued her mind: "Why me?"

She had committed her life to Christ as a young woman and years later had devoted herself to vocational ministry, and yet God *still* allowed terrible, soul-squelching suffering to enter her life. Had she done something wrong that warranted abusive treatment like that? Did God not care about her at all?

One afternoon during a counseling session, my friend stopped Jane mid-conversation and asked, "Jane, where do you suppose Jesus was when you were being abused?"

There was silence in response.

"Jane," she continued, "I'd like for you to take some time this week and ask Jesus where he was during those times when your husband was beating you up. Ask him to show you specifically—literally—where he was while you were being hurt. Come back to me once you receive an answer so that we can talk about what you find out."

Jane did exactly what she had been asked to do. During a private time that week, she went before God in prayer and allowed herself mentally to go back to those episodes when she was being struck by a belt at her husband's hand, and then asked, "Jesus, where were you then?"

She paused and waited for his reply. The picture that then came to mind was of Jesus standing right there in the room beside her husband and her, tears of grief streaming down his holy face. Receiving that image proved to be a major tipping point in Jane's process of healing, because she realized in that moment of reflection that she had not been abandoned, as she had once so firmly believed.

This is the gist of Psalm 23:4, which we looked at in chapter 3. When we walk through the darkest of valleys, we don't need to fear any evil because "you are with me," the psalmist declares. "Your rod and your staff, they comfort me."

Even during those times when we don't detect God's presence, we must cling to the knowledge that he is there. But simultaneously we must also acknowledge that he can and does choose to allow suffering to unfold. Yes, suffering grows us up in Christlike maturity, but it serves a deeper purpose than that. Suffering reminds us that we are still living in the old order of things, that while heaven is coming to earth, it is not *fully* here just yet. This truth is evidenced by every drunk-driving accident, drug-induced gang fight, and domestic-abuse incident that occurs. It is proven out every time another child is sold into sex slavery, every time a war breaks out somewhere in the world: we are caught between the Garden of Eden and heaven, the pristine dwelling we desperately crave.

Revelation 21 offers an attractive description of what this new order will include. There the apostle John wrote,

> Then I saw a new heaven and a new earth, for the first heaven and the first earth had passed away, and there was no longer any sea. I saw the Holy City, the new Jerusalem, coming down out of heaven from God, prepared as a bride beautifully dressed for her husband. And I heard a loud voice from the throne saying, "Now the dwelling of God is with men, and he will live with them. They will be his people, and God himself will be with them and be their God. He will wipe every tear from their eyes. There will be no more death or mourning or crying or pain, for the old order of things has passed away."
>
> —*Revelation 21:1–4*

So, yes, a fantastic new order is making its way to us. But it has not arrived in full. And if you're like me, there are days here on planet Earth when you are very aware of that fact. Some days bear the fragrance of heaven, but some days are of the old-order type. December 9 was one of those days. If there was a place where Jesus should have been hanging out on December 9, 2007, it was at New Life Church. He knew *full well* what was about to happen, and yet tragedy *still* struck our church.

After a day like that, you and I must hold fast to the Word of God. "He made known to us the mystery of his will according to his good pleasure," promises Ephesians 1:9–10, "which he purposed in Christ, to be put into effect when the times will have reached their fulfillment —to bring all things in heaven and on earth together under one head, even Christ." In other words, the kingdom of God has come, but not yet. And until that grand fulfillment unfolds in our midst, we wait and crave and groan, as Romans 8:22–23 says, like a mom waiting for her baby to be born. We eagerly anticipate our full adoption; we wait for our bodies to be fully redeemed.

In the days and weeks following the shooting, the other leaders at New Life and I made a concerted effort not only to reset our own expectations regarding pain and suffering in this life but also to remind those we lead that there is a graceful and God-honoring way to mourn even gut-wrenching loss. We encouraged them to keep their commitment to Christ, to confront their pain head-on, to remember that we are still living in the old order of things here on earth. But there was another aspect to finding healing in those early days, which was to prepare ourselves for the next season of suffering that someday would surely emerge.

As human beings, our tendency is to adopt a reactive approach to suffering. In New York City, 9/11 happens, for instance, and pastors and churchgoers all over the country spend weeks on end trying to soothe each other from the shock of what has just erupted in their world.

But what if, instead of reacting to an event like that, we *prepared* to face tough times? Imagine what would have occurred if Christ followers had talked for five or six years straight about episodes of persecution in the Bible and how we as lovers of God would most likely be persecuted someday too. Imagine if pastors had prepared their people for the arrival of a very dark day, a day that would have the potential to alter the face of our country forever.

Just as Jesus prepared his disciples in John 14–16 for the suffering they inevitably would face, we can commit to doing the same, both for ourselves and for those we lead. Yes, we should teach what Jesus says about contentment, abundance, and success. But we must also deal with the parts of the Bible that say, "Bad things will happen to you." Yes, we should emphasize the "rich, better, healthy" aspects of marriage—but we must also acknowledge the poor, worse, sick part of the deal. Yes, we should celebrate the job that was landed, the raise that was secured, the house that sold, the health report that came back clean, the baby that was finally conceived. But we must also show up in grace and truth when the parent dies, the economy dips, the car wreck occurs, and life comes crashing down. We must remind people that God has not fled the scene. He is aware of all that is going on, and one day he will make every wrong right. But that day is not yet here. Until then we are to claim the victory that Jesus secured for us on the cross and hang on to the hope that remains ours in him.

In his book *After You Believe*, Bible scholar N. T. Wright says, "God's future is arriving in the present, in the person and work of Jesus Christ, and you can practice, right now, the habits of life which will find their goal in that coming future."[3] Wright goes on to explain that those habits or practices center on seeking not happiness but *blessedness* in the course of our daily lives. "'Happiness' is simply a state of being for a human, as a self-contained unit," says the author. "You might, in principle, attain it on your own and develop it for your own sake. 'Blessedness,' however, is what happens when the creator God is at work both *in* someone's life and *through* that person's life."[4]

We'll further explore this idea of consecration—being set apart for God's use—in the next chapter. But as it relates to the concept of squaring our theology with God's perspective on things—namely that the Christian life is not a perpetual Disney experience and that suffering must run its course—let me say this: when our attention is fixed solely on reflecting God's work in and through our lives, all lesser goals fade to gray.

I'll show you what I mean.

Luke 18:35–42 tells the story of a blind beggar who receives his sight:

As Jesus approached Jericho, a blind man was sitting by the roadside begging. When he heard the crowd going by, he asked what was happening. They told him, "Jesus of Nazareth is passing by."

He called out, "Jesus, Son of David, have mercy on me!"

Those who led the way rebuked him and told him to be quiet [ironic, isn't it, that they didn't want someone desperately in need of healing disturbing the greatest Healer the world would ever know], but he shouted all the more, "Son of David, have mercy on me!"

Jesus stopped and ordered the man to be brought to him. When he came near, Jesus asked him, "What do you want me to do for you?"

"Lord, I want to see," he replied.

Jesus said to him, "Receive your sight; your faith has healed you." Immediately he received his sight and followed Jesus, praising God. When all the people saw it, they also praised God.

The blind beggar's interaction with the Son of God intrigues me every time I read it. He was close enough to Christ to have his request heard, he was bold enough in his faith to ask Christ for healing, he was steadfast enough in his belief to know that Christ could meet his need, and in response to Jesus having mercy on him, he followed and praised the Lord.

I think there is a lesson here for us to learn.

During these days when we are stuck between the now and the not yet, will we also lean closer to Christ? Despite the seasons of suffering that we'll certainty be asked to endure, will we stick to the commitment we've made to him? Our trials can either grow us up or get us down. Only we can choose how we'll respond.

I remember wanting to be matured as a result of my pain in the days after the shooting. I would pray to God, not so much for me to make sense of the suffering but for me to empty the contents of a contaminated soul. I was weary and confused and frustrated that healing seemed to be hiding from me. But with each interaction I realized that God was leading me one step closer to feeling whole. His attentiveness to my need—not to mention his unparalleled listening—compelled me to keep my commitment to him, the commitment to serve him all of my days.

Then, like the beggar, will we too be bold enough in our faith to keep making our request before God? Will we hang on to hope for healing—as the beggar did, believing from his toes all the way to his functionless eyes that Jesus could meet his need—even when evidence all around us seems to point to the terrible, old order of things? Ephesians 1:3 promises that we have already been blessed in the heavenly realms "with every spiritual blessing in Christ." If you belong to Christ, ultimate healing is yours. The issue that remains is whether you'll live as though that is true.

God's Word is replete with examples of Jesus' unparalleled ability to heal. Luke 4:40 says, "When the sun was setting, the people brought to Jesus all who had various kinds of sickness, and laying his hands on each one, he healed them." Later in Luke, we read this: "He went down with [the twelve disciples] and stood on a level place. A large crowd of his disciples was there and a great number of people from all over Judea, from Jerusalem, and from the coast of Tyre and Sidon, who had come to hear him and to be healed of their diseases. Those troubled by evil spirits were cured, and the people all tried to touch him, because power was coming from him and healing them all" (Luke 6:17–19).

Now, either the power that Jesus showcased that day still exists, or it doesn't. Either Jesus remains the same in nature today as he was back then, or he doesn't. Which is it?

The answer of course is that Jesus is the same yesterday, today, and forever (Heb. 13:8). The healing power he carried with him as he ministered here on earth is the same power he is willing to wield in your life and in mine. Will we cling to that belief, even when suffering has its way?

I have prayed for people whose tumors miraculously disappeared, and I have prayed for those who died the very next day. I've seen God restore people's financial stability, and I've seen bankruptcy papers filed. I've watched our heavenly Father heal a marriage in crisis, and I've watched as young kids cried while their parents divided assets and said their goodbyes. It's a rush to witness those good times, but what do you do with the bad?

Author Randy Alcorn tells the story of a man who lost his faith after a terrible season of suffering and pain. "My heart breaks for him," Alcorn writes, "and I pray that my family and I will never suffer what he did." Then Alcorn makes this profound statement: "But if personal suffering gives sufficient evidence that God doesn't exist, then surely I shouldn't wait until *I* suffer to conclude he's a myth. If *my* suffering would one day justify denying God, then I should deny him now in light of *other* people's suffering."[5]

In my own life, I have known the pain of crushing circumstances and the elation of very good days. But through the suffering as well as the joy, I can see how it all has matured me in Christ. I can look back on the journey thus far and see reflected in every step that this place is not my home, that heaven has come, but not fully yet. And from the victories God has given me, I can gain strength to keep fighting a very worthy fight.

You and I are engaged in a substantial battle every day of our lives. And in order for us to prevail, we've got to reset our expectations about this thing called life. God is not a myth, and his power has not waned. There is purpose in our suffering, and thankfully heaven will one day be our home. Until then, lean into your God. Make plain your requests. Reaffirm your belief that he is able to provide for your every need. And invest yourself wholeheartedly in praising his glorious name. This is how we cooperate in God's work to take back territory from the enemy until the day when heaven fully comes to earth.

CHAPTER 6

The Only Time We Can Worship God Is Now

The reason why many are still troubled,
still seeking, still making little forward progress
is because they haven't yet come to the end
of themselves. We're still trying to give orders,
and interfering with God's work within us.
—*A. W. Tozer*

IN THE DAYS AFTER THE SHOOTING, MINISTRY AT NEW LIFE STILL NEEDED to go on. But those of us responsible for leading, serving, and communicating with the congregation were shell-shocked, empty, and numb. New Life has always been a worshiping church, a group of believers determined to be presence-led by the Holy Spirit rather than performance-led by human beings. I once heard that if you don't teach people to worship, you'll have to entertain them every week. Thankfully, New Lifers knew well how to worship. It wasn't entertainment they sought Sunday after Sunday; it was the unparalleled presence of God.

We had worshiped God faithfully before the shooting, and I felt sure we would worship him consistently again. The only question that remained was whether we'd also choose to worship him now, when everything felt heavy and sad.

Exactly two weeks before the shooting—on November 25, 2007 —Ross Parsley delivered a sermon to our church titled "Worship Your Way through It: Finding God in Difficult Times." Referencing the words of Psalm 13, Ross made the observation that the only way David could have begun a psalm with griping, "How long, O LORD? Will you forget me *forever?*... How long must I wrestle with my thoughts and every day have sorrow in my heart?" (Ps. 13:1–2, emphasis added) and ended gratefully, "But I trust in your unfailing love; my heart rejoices in your salvation. I will sing to the LORD, for he has been good to me" (vv. 5–6), was that he had learned how to *worship* his way through tough times.

"Worship is believing that God has answers when we don't," Ross said. "It is fixing our eyes on Jesus instead of on our troubling circumstances, focusing not on the problem but on the author of the solution. Worship is giving thanks to God even before the long-awaited resolution makes itself known."

Ross couldn't possibly have known at the time how prophetic his words would be, given the events that would unfold fourteen short days later, but as our staff sought to find our footing after that December ordeal, it was the concepts Ross had presented during his talk that kept us tethered to our worshiping roots.

Slowly but surely, in small staff gatherings and congregational worship services alike, as a church we agreed—through words, through prayers, through song—that we needed God's intervention in new and profound ways. Collectively, we had been emptied; creatively, things felt dry. We didn't have the same spark of energy that had accompanied life before December 9. The chorus we sing that says to God, "I'm desperate for you," expressed *precisely* how we felt.

And so we took Ross and the great God he was pointing us to at their word. We fought the desire to put all our attention on the situation at hand: namely, that a year after one horrible scandal had struck, a gunman had stolen our innocence and killed two girls whom we loved. Instead, we looked to the One who knew the good plans he was purposing as a result of those tragic events.

Years ago I learned that one of the keys to my staying connected to God was simply to "mutter" to him all day long, not complaining but rather candidly verbalizing my feelings during the course of my day. Throughout many seasons of my journey following Christ, I'd mutter to God my thoughts about everything from big and important events about to occur in my life to the most mundane details of a typical workday afternoon.

I remember muttering a lot during those tumultuous mid-December days after the shooting. At that time, however, my muttering had more to do with a constant cry for help. I thought about how deeply I desired protection for us as a body, and healing for those who had been hurt physically, emotionally, or both. I considered how grateful I was that more damage hadn't been done. I told God how much I craved his presence, his power, his unparalleled peace. I muttered my need for his wisdom and for direction on how to lead the people of New Life when I myself was in pain. "Lead me on your paths of righteousness right now," I'd plead before God. "Be my Shepherd. Be my guide. Show me where to plant my next step. Give me grace as I walk this path."

As December gave way to January, I realized I had muttered my way into a new year. I thought back to when I had started that habit decades prior, and then muttered to God how thankful I was that the practice was serving me so well. That's the thing about a crisis: it reveals who you already are. Tough times may shape character over time, but initially they merely reveal what character you already have. If you're a mutterer before a crisis hits, the crisis will reveal exactly what it is you're muttering about. And if you're an authentic worshiper of God *before* trials come your way, then despite the initial onslaught of conflicting emotions when tragedy strikes, which thrust you like a pinball from pain to doubt to confusion and back to pain again, you will eventually be compelled to turn to God with praise on your lips, peace in your heart, and confidence in your gaze.

One of my core beliefs was affirmed in the wake of Matthew Murray's attack on our church, which is that facades don't survive severe trauma. My southern-born grandmother — my mom's mom — used to say it this way: "When you're shaken, what's really inside of you will come spilling out."

When you and I get shaken by circumstances, when our lives are turned upside down, what's truest of us will come pouring out, in the same way that it's nearly impossible to keep an overfull cup of coffee contained when you find yourself doing thirty over a speed bump. Life's most jolting speed bumps reveal our innermost beliefs, the core of who we are.

Before I went to New Life to serve as senior pastor, my friend Tom Lane encouraged me to spend some time writing down my deeply held values. I'm sure his counsel was given at least partly because I was going through something of a midlife crisis: I had just turned forty, my dad had recently died, and I was leaving the staff of Gateway Church, a group I had come to genuinely love. It was all happening in one fell swoop, and what my wise friend knew was that if I didn't slow down, step away from sharp objects, and consider the truth of who Brady Boyd was, I'd probably cause someone harm. Most likely myself.

I still have the journal entry I started that day in answer to the question, "What is true about me?" It took me nearly three months to pray through and answer that single inquiry, but eventually I would compile a draft that accurately reflects what I am serious about, what I am passionate about, what I am devoted to, and what I absolutely will not negotiate away. How grateful I am to Tom for steering me toward that exercise; I had no idea how badly I'd need to know myself just three brief months into my new role.

* * *

Several hours after the shooting, it was apparent to me that the media frenzy that had kicked in immediately after the 911 calls were made from frantic New Lifers wasn't going to die down anytime soon. Our church had been the focus of many front-page stories for more than a year because of Ted Haggard's departure; the shooting added fuel to an already active fire.

As I mentioned in chapter 1, I found out mere minutes before my first press conference that I was due to address the reporters gathered outside our main building. As I headed out from my office, one of my associates asked, "Do you know what you're going to say?"

The answer, of course, was no. I was still shocked, stunned, and fighting to understand all that had just happened on our campus. But interestingly, as I neared the hundred or so reporters from major outlets like CNN and Fox News, I felt utterly at peace. It occurred to me during the thirty-second walk from my office to that media pool that while I didn't know exactly what I would say to those reporters, I knew decisively *who I was*. Which was a good thing, given that trying to sort out the real you half a minute before dozens of microphones are thrust in your face is a pretty ambitious goal.

"I am a child of God and am still safely in the palm of his hand," I thought as I approached the pool. Nothing could snatch me away from my Father's love, and regardless of what had transpired that day, my God remained in control. With our heavenly Father's unparalleled presence and power, somehow we'd all find our way through.

I stepped forward, offered my heartfelt comments to the reporters, and walked away from that press conference incredibly relieved that the nonnegotiables of my life had been nailed down long before. Facing a crisis is never fun, but facing one when you're still unsure of who you really are is a fate that feels worse than death. I learned that lesson the hard way, when I was just a sophomore in high school.

During my growing-up years, I was a huge basketball fan. I loved playing the game, talking about it, and watching it on TV. A bigger Boston Celtics fan couldn't be found in all of northern Louisiana, and the only thing I wanted to do once I hit high school age was to play for our town's most celebrated sports team, the Simsboro High Tigers. Our school was too small to have a football team, so the community structured their social life around basketball instead. Every boy raised in Simsboro had hoop dreams on his mind.

I'd had a heart condition since childhood, but during my freshman year of high school, I worked out a deal with my coach that allowed me to take breaks whenever I felt winded, and extra precautions when I was getting weak. He and I both knew my limitations, but he seemed to think my situation was worth accommodating because of the value I brought to the team. I was no Michael Jordan, but for a small kid from a small town, I'd say I held my own.

As I entered my sophomore year, officials from the state of Louisiana decided to enact tougher standards on the physical exams used to determine which kids could play sports and which could not. There had been talk about the dangers associated with exposing heart patients to the rigors of demanding sports such as basketball, and they didn't want to assume such high risk. Actually, their concerns would be warranted in the end: a few years later a star shooter from Loyola Marymount died during practice one day because of an enlarged heart.

But none of that was on my mind as I showed up for my physical, copies of the required medical records in hand. All I wanted to do was play basketball, regardless of how risky it seemed to anonymous officials I'd never met.

I flew through the physical and felt fine about my chances, but a week later my coaches and parents decided it was not safe for me to play. I had hopes of being a starter, and yet now I wouldn't be playing at all. My fifteen-year-old mind whirred with the injustice of it all. How come everyone *else* had been given a good heart, and I was stuck with one that was flawed? "Why won't you let me play?" I remember pleading with God.

In the end, I was so desperate to somehow be associated with the team that I volunteered to become team manager, the guy responsible for washing players' uniforms after practice and handing out water bottles during games. Obviously, it was no consolation for a young man whose dreams all centered on playing the game he loved. Basketball had been my idol, and God had allowed that idol to fall.

The experience broke me. And because I didn't particularly like the feeling of being broken, I made a vow before God: "I'm done," I told him, with arrogance to spare. "Whatever I believed about you before, I now no longer believe."

I had been pretty interested in the things of God at that young age, but from that moment until my senior year of college, I determinedly moved away from him. I was so angry for what God had allowed to happen to me that I wanted nothing to do with him anymore.

It was during that seven-year span of blatant rebellion that I invested myself in "better" ways. Who needed God when I could instead have more fun drinking enough to float a battleship? In addition, I smoked everything I could find to smoke, I became incredibly immoral with my body, and I threw away every last care I'd held. If God wasn't going to look after me, then I'd better learn to look after myself. So I did. And I watched myself walk right into near-addiction before I realized the idiocy of my self-focused ways.

At fifteen, I hadn't yet confirmed my commitment to Christ. I hadn't resolved in my heart to *worship* God, regardless of what circumstances came my way. I hadn't established my nonnegotiables, those things that were truest about God and about me. And when crisis erupted in my young, teenage life, it nearly did me in. Without a clear understanding that being committed to God means being set apart for his purposes, which might sometimes clash with my own, I sank in the quicksand I'd chosen to stand on.

I've seen the same dynamic play out in painful living color with countless couples over the years, especially those who have suffered the death of a child. The marriage is fragile to begin with, the loss of a child occurs, and the couple simply can't rally the emotional resolve to put things back together again. They never took the time to lay out their agreed-upon nonnegotiables, and once they found themselves in crisis, they realized they had no foundation on which to stand.

Back at New Life, during the weeks and months after tragedy struck, I reminded our staff members and congregation alike that we have a very real enemy in this world and that his only job is to steal, kill, and destroy. "Our hope is opposed," I told them. "Our healing is opposed. Our health is opposed. Every good thing God hopes to accomplish as a result of what we've just walked through is *vehemently* opposed by Satan."

An effective way to combat his attacks, I told them, was for us to worship our way through the pain, the suffering, the disillusionment, the sadness, the darkness, the bleakness, the grief. "We can't cling to powerful worship experiences from the past," I said. "And we can't simply wait for the skies to clear up and the sun to start shining before we'll commit to authentically worshiping God again. The only time we can worship is now. And *worship* is what we must do."

Through the years, I have had dozens of conversations with Christ followers about what it looks like to *really* worship God. The Bible is filled with ideas for how to answer this question, but let me give you three themes that rose to the surface for our church.

First, to become authentic worshipers, our congregation realized that we had to stay current with God. Again and again Scripture demonstrates this pattern of living in constant communion with God: "My soul yearns for you in the night," Isaiah 26:9 says. "In the morning my spirit longs for you." "Earnestly I seek you," writes David in Psalm 63. "My soul thirsts for you, my body longs for you, in a dry and weary land where there is no water.... On my bed I remember you; I think of you through the watches of the night" (Ps. 63:1, 6). And then in Psalm 34:1, "I will extol the LORD at all times; his praise will always be on my lips."

You can't read the pages of Scripture without seeing the common refrain of worship equating to *constant connection with God*. His true followers crave his presence and power, and they spend their days and nights straining after God. And for good reason: 2 Chronicles 16:9 says that a great reward awaits those who diligently seek the Lord. "The eyes of the LORD range throughout the earth *to strengthen those* whose hearts are fully committed to him" (emphasis added). Divine strength for our seasons of struggle — who wouldn't want an infusion like that?

I encourage pastors, church workers, and everyday followers of Christ to be sure that whatever ministry they are providing in this world is happening from the overflow of their cup, not from the dregs that linger down at the bottom. God is looking for worshipers who are faithfully staying current with him, not those who try to fake fresh.

A second means of becoming authentic worshipers of God that we learned at New Life is to simply mean what we sing. Pastor and author A. W. Tozer once said, "Christians don't tell lies; they just go to church and sing them."[6] It's sobering, but I've often found it to be true.

I took the platform one Sunday recently at New Life in the middle of our opening song set and said, "We've been singing together for more than half an hour now. Do you truly mean the words that you sing?" I think the song we had just sung was "Counting on God," a terrific declaration written by one of our worship leaders, Jared Anderson. But if we say we are counting on God for our joy and our strength and our solid-rock faith, as the song says, and in fact are not counting on him for these things, then something is terribly wrong.

I told our congregation that it would be far better for us to stand silently than to proclaim to God something we didn't actually believe. And I offered to be the first among us to follow that advice. "I commit to you afresh that I will not sing one more song unless I mean the words of that song to my core."

Authentic worshipers of God stand behind the words they speak, the words they pray, and the words they choose to sing.

A third way to become authentic worshipers of God is to carefully guard our hearts. *The Message* paraphrase of Proverbs 4:23 puts it this way: "Keep vigilant watch over your heart; that's where life starts." Or check out the Contemporary English Version's adaptation, which makes plain that the heart in question is our *emotional* heart, the epicenter of our thought life: "Carefully guard your thoughts because they are the source of true life."

Contrary to popular opinion, the gospel is an inside-out work. We try to make it outside-in by racking up good deeds in a futile attempt to impress others and God. But that's not at all how it works. Throughout Scripture, God as much as says, "Come to me and let me love you first. Then I'll equip you for every good work you seek to do." What's more, we find in Romans 12:2 that the only way we get to know what God's will is for our lives is to be transformed by the renewing of our minds. "Then you will be able to test and approve what God's will is — his good, pleasing and perfect will."

If we crave genuine communion with God — *authentic* worship — and if we desire to know his perfect will for our lives so we then can plant our footsteps in it, then we must first take every thought captive and steer it right back toward him.

I'll explain why.

As I said, Satan vehemently opposes every good thing God wants to accomplish in and through our lives — but that doesn't explain how he goes about his evil schemes. So here it is: Satan's attacks always involve hijacking part of our thought life and working to convince us that a lie is somehow true.

As I mentioned earlier, one of the pervasive lies floating around New Life after Matthew Murray's rampage was that our best days were behind us. Things felt so sorrowful and dark that in unguarded moments it was easy for us to cave to lies such as, "It will always feel this bleak" or "God must be mad at us" or "Nobody will want to worship at New Life anymore." The lies sometimes feel safer than the truth, because we resonate deeply with them in our flesh. Like a person downing hot soup on a cold day, our souls lap up what seems on the surface to articulate how we're really feeling. But in the end, we are forced to face the truth: our flesh deceives us terribly. Amid seasons of struggle, what *seems* like the truth is often a lie shot straight from the pit of hell. Which is why we must be diligent, as 2 Corinthians 10:5 says, to "demolish arguments and every pretension that sets itself up against the knowledge of God." And the way we get that done, the verse continues, is by taking "captive every thought to make it obedient to Christ."

Let me make this concept painfully practical by putting it in the context of marriage for a moment.

Over the years, I have counseled countless couples whose marriages were teetering on the brink of divorce. And in the vast majority of those cases, sadly, an affair was at the center of the dissension. It didn't take long for me to notice a trend with these couples. In every single situation where an extramarital affair had occurred, three specific steps always led to the philanderer's demise. These three may not seem profound, but they certainly are true.

First, something made the person lean away from his or her marriage. The culprit could be as seemingly innocuous as he forgetting to take out the garbage again, or she nagging him about his late work hours again, or he failing to manifest a little romance again, or she blabbing family-only information to her girlfriends one more time. Whatever the situation was, it caused one or both members of the couple to subtly lean away. That's step number one.

Step two occurs when the wandering mate then becomes aware of another person. And third, he or she begins to flirt with that newer, "more exciting" person.

That's it—three simple steps that can lead to years of great pain, because as you'd guess, there are many more steps that inevitably follow, including secret encounters and a thick and tragic web of deceit.

But as I have sat across from those couples in crisis, here is what has intrigued me every time: what adulterous spouses never seemed to grasp up front was that as early as step two—when they simply formed an awareness of another person—they had officially begun negotiating with the Devil. Because it is in step two of that progression when Satan starts feeding us lies.

You married the wrong person, he quietly whispers.

You deserve to be happy.

Your current spouse will never make you happy.

You'd be much better off if you married that other person instead.

Satan, the skilled negotiator, comes along and points poisonous arrows like those right where he knows we are vulnerable. He knows by observation how we are wired and how we choose to run our lives. He knows our attitudes, our tendencies, our behaviors, our favorite sins. He knows the right buttons to push and *exactly* how to push them.

I speak from personal experience here. When I was in my mid-twenties, I was the target of Satan's taunts. He would come along periodically and whisper, *You know, Brady, you sure did get married young.*

Pam and I married when I was twenty-two and she was twenty-one. And in those early, sometimes tumultuous days of marriage when both of us were trying to sort out who we were as individuals and who we were going to be as a couple, I'd find myself listening to Satan's lies. *What if you had just waited a little while?* Satan would suggest. *Once you matured, you might have picked a totally different mate.* Sure enough, if I wasn't carefully guarding my heart in that moment, I would internalize the lies, I would subtly lean away from my marriage, and I would step unwittingly into territory that is dangerous at best.

Clearly, this warning applies to marital relationships, but it pertains to every other aspect of life as well: if we step into negotiations with the enemy, we are guaranteed to lose every time. Regardless of how strong, disciplined, or savvy you may be, you are no match for the master deceiver. The same is true of me. Satan has defeated women and men far wiser than we, and to think we can take him on is to prove ourselves absolute fools.

If you know anything about the card game Spades, then you know that the coveted ace of spades trumps every other card in the deck. If you find that card in your hand when the deck is dealt, your chances of winning the round are exponentially higher than those of the other players. Because of that, I keep an ace of spades playing card on my desk or tucked in my Bible at all times as a reminder that Jesus Christ holds that trump card in my life.

What I have noticed about Christians who self-destruct along the way is that at some point they figuratively gave Satan that card. They bought a lie, they ditched the truth, and they slid their ace of spades his way.

Surely, you have seen this happen too. A high-profile ministry leader seems to be doing everything right. He is gifted, he is gregarious, and he can really attract a crowd. Satan eyes the up-and-comer and says, *H'mmm, looks like that guy is building quite a bit of influence these days. If he keeps going, he is going to enjoy tremendous favor from God. But wait—well, would you look at that! He handed me his trump card, for me to use whenever I like. Well, I think I'll just pocket this for now and watch everything unfold for a while.*

Now, to be clear, Satan's decision to wait for things to unfold is not a function of patience. Patience is a fruit of the Spirit, and Satan is not Spirit-filled. But he *is* strategic. And while he cannot see our futures, as God can, he certainly can make out the horizon. He's something of a really good weatherman, you might say—someone who can pretty accurately forecast tomorrow based on what he's observing today.

And so Satan waits for the most strategic time, the time when his actions can wreak the most havoc, and then just when that Christ follower with a secret least expects it, Satan slaps down the winning card he's been given. The spade is played, the truth is exposed, and deception's walls come tumbling down.

Yes, the gospel is an inside-out work, but so is the work of darkness. You and I are designed to withstand every temptation, Scripture promises (1 Cor. 10:13)—*unless* we've given Satan a piece of our heart. If you want to become an authentic worshiper of God, guard your heart at every turn. It is the heart that brings forth the rest of life. It is our *heart* that declares whose we are.

As those of us who call New Life home upped again our commitment to authentically worship God—even in the midst of darkness, even when our hearts were sad—we noticed some undeniable benefits surface that blessed us deeply as a result.

Almost immediately after the start of the Wednesday night family meeting we held just days after the shooting, as the initial downbeat for the worship team's first song was played, I was refreshed in my understanding of how authentic worship always reminds us of what is true: God is still on his throne; Jesus Christ remains our loving, ever-present mediator; the Holy Spirit promises to intercede on our behalf, even when we're clueless about what to pray for or about the right words to use before God. These things are always *true*, but the chaos of crisis has a way of numbing us to that reality.

Another bit of truth we were tempted to forsake in our sadness and pain was that our essence is *spiritual*, not human, in nature. Someone wisely once said, "We are not human beings going through a temporary spiritual experience. We are spiritual beings going through a temporary human experience." Granted, we mustn't diminish what happens in and through our earthly bodies. We just need to remember that this fallen, worldly existence will not last forever; instead of becoming consumed with our fleshly pain, then, we are to stay laser-focused on the spiritual race we run. We are not settlers here on this earth; we are simply sojourners passing through. Engaging wholeheartedly in worshiping God helped bring us all back to that truth.

As a church, we also benefited from the recharging of batteries that happens when a person worships God. Worshiping is an act of *submission* to God. It's a declaration that his ways really are better than ours.

It is an opportunity for us to be emptied and then beautifully refilled by him. In a marvelous exchange, worship allows mortal humans to lay down question marks, doubts, concerns, and fears and pick up pure freedom instead.

You and I both have several internal batteries that determine how much energy is available for us to expend on our involvements in life. When these batteries are fully charged, we can take on multiple kingdom-oriented tasks and accomplish each of them well. But when those batteries are nearing depletion, even routine parts of life feel hard.

For example, we have a *spiritual* battery that gets charged only as we connect with God through worship and prayer. We have a *work* battery that supplies energy to do the job God has called each of us to do. We charge that battery when we say yes to the things we should be doing and no to those we should not. We charge that battery when we operate in our God-given strength and calling and when we give him the praise for successes we see.

If you have children, then there is a *parent* battery that gets charged only by quality time spent connecting with your kids. Abram and Callie are eleven and nine, and at this stage of their lives, they require a lot of my time. What this means is that I can't devote 100 percent of my passion and energy to New Life, come home each night with an empty tank, and expect to pass myself off as a great dad. So during the twelve-minute drive from the church to my house, I unplug my work battery and start revving up the dad battery, in anticipation of giving myself over fully to those I am called to raise.

In the same vein, if you are married, then there is a *spouse* battery that absolutely must stay charged. There have been seasons of my life when I have neglected this battery more than all of the other three combined, but thankfully, Pam has been gracious with me as I have renewed my commitment to giving her my best time, my best energy, my best self. After all, the last thing I want to do is to neglect connecting with the one person I love most.

Not surprisingly, as we as a church committed ourselves to authentically worshiping God—with our words, with our prayers, with our songs—we found that our energy for *all* of life soared.

Ready for a third benefit to genuine worship? Coming before God continuously in a posture of humility and with abundant praise on our lips invites him to steady our stance so we will be prepared to endure future seasons of pain.

I realize this doesn't sound like much of a benefit. Who wants to do *anything* that would possibly invite future pain? But as we saw in chapter 5, we are already guaranteed some tough times in this life, and you and I both would do well to step into those episodes with as sure-footed a stance as possible.

Psalm 18:31 – 33 says, "Who is God besides the LORD? And who is the Rock except our God? It is God who arms me with strength and makes my way perfect. He makes my feet like the feet of a deer; he enables me to stand on the heights." Those words took on new meaning to me after the shooting. It was as if God himself said, *Brady, I never promised that the path would be free of rocks or treachery. But I did promise to give you the feet of a deer.* Undeniably, on December 9, 2007, my wide, pleasant path became difficult, narrow, and steep. But God immediately kept his word to me—he made me as sure-footed as a deer.

The deer described in the Old Testament are not the elegant whitetails I grew up hunting in the woods of northwest Louisiana, but the point is exactly the same: all deer were distinctly designed by God to be able to bound across treacherous paths with balance, agility, and grace. I've been to the desert south of Jerusalem where the psalmist David used to tend his father's flock of sheep, and whenever I read the words of Psalm 18, I imagine him standing at the bottom of a hill and eyeing the huge cliffs above. Seeing the craggy surfaces, the severe drop-offs, the series of tightly woven switchbacks that years of hoofmarks have carved into the ground, he must have marveled all over again that any animal could negotiate such terrain without stumbling.

Throughout the state of Colorado, there are many mountainous roads that wind across steep passes and breathtaking drop-offs. Invariably, when I'm driving through the most harrowing parts, I'll look up and see a bunch of deer or bighorn sheep meandering around as if they were standing on flat Texas soil. They graze on patches of earth that seem no bigger than a silver dollar and look down at you as if to say, "What? You call *this* tight?"

Lately, whenever I see those impossibly agile beasts, I remember David's words to us. "Don't become so consumed with the landscape that you forget that your footing is sure," I think he is saying through the ideas of that psalm. "You're steadier than you think when you choose to trust God with your stance."

Less than one year following the shooting, I would discover why God was intent on reminding me to take my eyes off my craggy surroundings and instead trust him with my footing. On a Wednesday night in November 2008, I got one of those dreaded phone calls at 4:00 a.m., a call you instinctively know does not carry good news. I answered and moments later learned that my nineteen-year-old nephew, Austin, had been killed in a car wreck just outside of Baton Rouge.

Within hours I had boarded a plane bound for Louisiana, where I would remain by my sister's side for the balance of the week.

Throughout his entire life, Austin had resembled me so closely that most strangers thought he was not my nephew but my son. Little Brady, everyone called him, a moniker he seemed to wear with pride. Days before he died, Pam and the kids and I had spent the Thanksgiving holiday at my sister's house, and the afternoon before we headed back to Colorado, I spent two hours in the front yard throwing a football with Austin and catching up on his life. As I packed my bag to head to his funeral, my arm was still sore from those throws.

My reaction to the news was to deny that the worst had occurred.

He hadn't even made it to age twenty! He had *so* much life left to live. But before the swirl of useless declarations continued, I sensed God capturing my thoughts. *I know this isn't where you thought you'd be standing today,* he said, *but I'll help you stay steady through this.*

God had taught me a lot about trusting him in the eleven months that had just come and gone, and I knew that by his strength, I'd stand.

There has been a fourth benefit that we at New Life Church have relished as a result of choosing to adopt a posture of authentic worship before God, and it is this: when we worship our way through crises, we reveal something of our powerful and loving Creator to a curious, watching world.

I've often said that while people are *always* watching us as believers —to see how we act, how we react, how we serve a world desperately in need—there are two times when their eyes are especially peeled: they seem most keenly interested in our lives when we are experiencing the greatest amount of *success* and when we are experiencing the greatest amount of *hardship.*

As I engaged in interviews with high-profile media outlets in the days immediately following the shooting, I was reminded of Psalm 31:19, which says this, speaking of God: "How great is the goodness you have stored up for those who fear you. You lavish it on those who come to you for protection, blessing them before the watching world" (NLT).

That verse played itself out in interesting ways. For instance, during my interview with Larry King, he asked, "So, Pastor Boyd, does this terrible event that has just happened to your church shake your faith at all?" And as I answered him—"No, of course it doesn't. It only confirms that what I believe is true"—I thought, "How incredible is this, God! The secular media is offering me a perfect platform from which to share your power and love."

Yes, we had faced awful circumstances that had us clamoring to

God for protection. But we had not been deserted by our heavenly Father, and now he was using that same situation to *bless* us before a watching world. He was causing all things to work together for good (Rom. 8:28), bringing himself fully deserved glory in the end.

Prior to its official release a few years ago, I was able to see a sneak preview of the independent documentary titled *Expelled: No Intelligence Allowed*, hosted by political commentator Ben Stein. In it, Stein interviews a man who is perhaps the most famous atheist on the planet. In one of the man's books, which has sold millions of copies around the world, he writes this: "The God of the Old Testament is arguably the most unpleasant character in all fiction. Jealous and proud of it. A petty, unjust, unforgiving control-freak. A vindictive, blood-thirsty ethnic cleanser. A misogynistic, homophobic, racist, infanticidal, genocidal, filicidal, pestilential, megalomaniacal, fatalistic, capriciously malevolent bully."[7]

During a one-on-one interview with the author, Stein decides to follow up on that quote. After reciting it verbatim, he meets the atheist's eyes and says, rather hypothetically and with a winsome look on his face, "I'm just curious here, but what if, after you died, you ran into God and heard him say, 'What have you been *doing*? I mean, I've been trying to be nice to you.... I gave you a multimillion-dollar paycheck over and over again with your book deals ... and look what you did!"

The atheist, now laughing at the good-natured intent of the question, says in response, "Bertrand Russell had that point put to him, and he said something like [speaking to God], 'Sir, why did you take such pains to hide yourself?'"

I watched that clip, got to the end, and watched it in its entirety again. The thought that crossed my mind was this: "If God ever is hard to find, it is because he is hard to find in us, his followers, those who say they have surrendered their lives to him."

God's job description contains only one task — to spread his own glory throughout the earth — and the way he gets that job done is through believers like you and me. That's it. That's his grand plan. And there is no plan B in the works.

This is why Scripture is so clear in telling us that we are salt and light in this often tasteless and dreary world (Matt. 5:13 – 14). It's also why we are told never to put our light — the evidence of our faith in Christ — under a bowl or keep it hidden in any way (Matt. 5:15 – 16). Jesus intends to shine himself *through* us, which is a key means by which others find God.

As I considered the atheist's response to Stein's question, I resolved then and there to walk through the aftermath of an admittedly terrible tragedy in a way that would make it *easy* for others to see God. I wasn't resolving to be churchy or religious. In fact, that's probably the worst thing I could have done. Our culture spots posers quickly; wearing a mask of piety or religiosity when onlookers knew I was dealing with great pain would have instantly outed me as a fraud.

What I *was* resolving was to be authentic in my worship and candid about the source of my strength. The process since then hasn't been perfect, but as recently as three weeks ago I saw clear proof that real progress is being made.

Our church hosts an early-morning prayer gathering for men in the Colorado Springs community a few times a week, and three weeks ago, on a Thursday morning when eighty or ninety men were gathered in the World Prayer Center to focus their lives on God, I closed out our time together with an unusual challenge.

I'd been compelled to make a change in my own life and wondered if a few of those guys would join me in my little experiment, just to see what God would do. "I need to be candid with you," I admitted from the front of the room. "Lately I feel like I spend more time intentionally tuning in to sports radio or the latest political pundit rant than I am spending tuned in to God."

I figured I wasn't alone in my slump, so I continued shooting straight.

"Judging by daily conversations I have around New Life, I think a few of you might be able to relate. And while ESPN Radio is a wonderful addition to life, in my view, if we're not extremely careful, we'll let ourselves be entertained away from God."

Without really thinking through the logistics of such an offer, I then explained to the men gathered there that I was going to spend a full week — from that Thursday until the following Friday morning — using every moment in my car to worship God instead of defaulting to the AM dial, and that if they wanted to join me in this challenge, I'd supply them free CDs to get the job done.

Thankfully, Pastor Lance Coles leaped up, rushed over to the main building, where a stash of New Life worship CDs are kept, and returned with a boxful of discs to hand out. We sell those same CDs every single week in our church's bookstore, but it had never occurred to the men in the room that *they* could benefit from a resource like that.

I've heard it said that as human beings, we are the sum total of the five biggest influences in our lives. For some it's family members. For some it's a boss. For some it's the drive to acquire as many toys as possible before the game is over. And for some it's whatever is happening on the radio when they're en route home after a long day. Considering the feedback I received from dozens of men the following week, I'd say an awful lot of good can be done in this world when the foremost among those influences is God. Following our drive-time experiment, men told me they were surprised by how contaminated and distracted their souls had become from the constant flow of political and sports-related banter. Once they allowed themselves a posture of worship during their daily commute, they remarked, their perspective shifted, their attitude improved, and they were automatically more focused on being the hands and feet of Christ in the world around them.

If you spend thirty minutes a day commuting back and forth to work, I guarantee that your perspective will shift too when you choose to devote that time to God. Talk to him, pray to him, sing to him, love him. Worship him in whatever way feels comfortable — just let *authenticity* guide your approach.

An old hymn says, "Turn your eyes upon Jesus / Look full in his wonderful face / And the things of earth will grow strangely dim / In the light of his glory and grace,"[8] which is *exactly* what happens when we make the choice to worship God. My bet is that there are a few things that could stand to grow dim in your life. And I know there are some in my life too.

In the wake of the shooting, I remember wanting things like buildings and titles and to-do lists to grow dim going forward. The more corporate side of church work felt so carnal and nauseating when contrasted with the fragility of life we'd just observed. Sure, it's nice to have a big building and expansive property and money in the bank. But those things hardly comprise the essence of this thing called life.

I don't want to define success by worldly things that one day will cease to exist. Instead, I want to measure it by how connected I am to God. Am I up to date with him? Do I mean the words I sing? Am I doing my best at every turn to faithfully guard my heart? Am I making it *easy* for others to see God? These are the questions I'm asking myself as I strive to be a more worshipful man. I hope you'll do the same.

In his brilliant book *Orthodoxy*, G. K. Chesterton wrote, "Man is more himself, man is more manlike, when joy is the fundamental thing in him, and grief the superficial. Melancholy should be an innocent interlude, a tender and fugitive frame of mind; praise should be the permanent pulsation of the soul."[9] In this life we *will* face hardship. But as we resurrender ourselves each time to the One who has overcome the world, that permanent, praise-filled pulsation can finally — and joyfully — be ours.

CHAPTER 7

Eventually You've Got to Get to the Giraffes

It is by those who have suffered
that the world has been advanced.
— Leo Tolstoy

IN THE SPRING OF 2009, A MAN FROM OUR FELLOWSHIP AND I MET FOR coffee. I had looked forward to getting to know him better after hearing what a great guy he is, but as we sat down at the coffee shop, he immediately said, "Brady, I have a word for you regarding the church."

I knew this conversation was quickly going deep. I didn't expect him to open our dialogue that way, but I often get prophetic words from people in our congregation and have been helped by enough of them to pay attention when they show up.

"I took my kids to the zoo last weekend," he continued, "and they absolutely loved it. Especially the lions. They just couldn't get enough of the lion exhibit. But after thirty minutes or so of staring at those lions, I was anxious to move on. Lions are great, but I was more than a little ready for something new."

He went on to explain that while he felt it was time to head to the next exhibit, his kids didn't exactly share his enthusiasm. "They refused to pry themselves away," he said. "So I decided just to leave."

His kids are young, so he didn't actually leave. But he pretended to head for the giraffe exhibit without them, making sure they saw him slowly walk away. "Hey, kids!" he cheered as he eased out of plain sight. "I'm heading for the giraffes. Want to come?"

At first his kids didn't buy it. Thinking that surely their caring and attentive father wouldn't abandon them, they stayed in front of the lions, their collective gaze fixed on each and every big-cat yawn. But within moments those lion lovers looked toward the giraffes, saw their dad heading for the excitement of a fresh exhibit, decided to ditch what they'd been staring at for well over half an hour, and rushed to catch up with the undisputed leader of their pack.

As we sat there huddled over cups of hot coffee, he said to me, "Brady, I think it's time that you help New Life get to the next exhibit. It has been a year and a half since the shooting, and I believe our people are ready to move ahead. Some of them may not *think* they're ready, but this much I guarantee: If you as our leader move on, the vast majority of the church will follow. If you leave the lions and head for the giraffes, we'll embrace a new exhibit too."

It was a perfect metaphor. Now all I had to do was sort out what New Life's next exhibit was to be.

Decades ago I was introduced to Elisabeth Kübler-Ross's "stages of grief" model from her book *On Death and Dying.*[10] She originally created it as a tool to help people suffering from terminal illness cope with the difficulties of knowing they were about to die. But over the last forty years, people have used it to work through almost any form of suffering—the death of a loved one, divorce, addiction, an infertility diagnosis, and more.

The first of five main stages that Kübler-Ross describes is *denial.* For example, you know you're in denial if you catch yourself after a tragic event saying, "No problem here. I feel just fine." Or, more obviously, "This can't really be happening to me." Denial is undoubtedly difficult, but at least it's a temporary state. A natural defense mechanism that shows up strong to protect the sufferer from exorbitant pain, denial typically gets swiftly replaced with a heightened state of awareness, both of the situation at hand and of the individuals who are being affected by it.

Stage two, she says, is *anger*. You're in this stage if you frequently play the "why me" card or spend an inordinate amount of energy trying to find someone to blame for your grief. The good news for you, if you're in stage two, is that you finally recognize that denial is doing you no favors. The *bad* news is that the denial you so tightly clung to tends to get replaced with less than pleasant emotions such as resentment, jealousy, and rage. Not fun.

Bargaining is the third stage of the grief cycle and is recognized by comments such as "I'll do *anything* if it will make this pain go away" or "Please, just let me live to see my grandchildren born." The bargaining stage brings with it the hope that you can somehow postpone pain or delay death. It involves making a plea with a higher power for more time, more health, more life, in exchange for a reformed lifestyle of some sort.

And then there is stage four, *depression*, in which a person's state of mind is reflected in such questions as, "Why bother living life, when I feel as sad as I do?" "I'm just going to die anyway, so what's the point of doing the laundry?" and "Why try to go on, when life has panned out like this?" During depression, people tend to isolate and insulate from the rest of the world. They cry. They grieve. They wonder how they're ever supposed to recover from whatever massive setback they've just endured. Grieving is actually good, says Kübler-Ross — as long as it doesn't last forever.

Assuming a person moves through all five stages of the cycle, *acceptance* finally shows up. "It's going to be okay," a person in this stage resolves. "The future doesn't have to be defined by the agonizing events of the past." And at this point, stage five of the grief model, a person is better able to take in the new reality that the suffering has introduced. Acceptance allows that person to move forward despite having once been paralyzed by great pain.

So, several hours after the shooting occurred, motivated by the desire to help our congregation reach stage-five living as quickly and yet humanely as possible, I called a pastor friend of mine who leads another church in Colorado Springs and asked if we could use his church's facilities as something of an off-site counseling headquarters for New Lifers who had witnessed the terrible events of the day, and if we could start as early as the very next morning. He gave a quick and heartfelt yes.

That Monday morning, more than one hundred crisis counselors showed up from all over the city. They volunteered their time for four days straight, and they helped scores of our people begin to work through their own cycles of pain.

The "stages of grief" concept was still fresh on my mind when, many months after the shooting, I was walking through New Life's foyer between Sunday morning services and was approached by a woman from our congregation, who asked if we could talk. She explained that although she knew intuitively that our church was a safe place to come and worship God, she still was having trouble getting thoughts of the shooting out of her mind. The culprit, she said, was the bundle of balloons being handed out in our children's ministry classes each weekend, a practice observed at New Life for years. "When I'm walking through the children's wing and one of those balloons happens to pop, I am reminded of the sound of gunfire, and I nearly come undone," she said. "Do you think we could forgo handing them out for a while — just until the rawness of the shooting isn't quite so raw anymore?"

I was so grateful for the woman's honesty. Working through grief's various cycles isn't the same for each of us. Some people move through the stages speedily, while others take their time. Some move from step one to step five, in sequential order. Others seem to take a circuitous route, shifting from step three to step four to step two to step one and then leapfrogging all the way to step five.

When the woman approached me that day, it was an instructive reminder to me that while I felt as though I'd already moved through the entire grief cycle by then, some members of our church were still hip-deep in very real pain. In addition to agreeing that we suspend until further notice the practice of distributing balloons, I also affirmed my commitment to meeting our people with compassion and understanding, right where they were.

If I had to point to one event that influenced how I coped with the grief my church and I felt after December 9, 2007, it would be the devastating loss of my dad.

When my dad was sixty years old, he discovered that he had colon cancer. Throughout his life he was a good man, but he never took care of himself on the diet-and-exercise front. Eventually cancer resulting from his poor habits spread to his liver, and this most likely is what finally took his life.

Spiritually, while Dad was never the passionate, talk-about-God-all-the-time kind of guy, he definitely had settled the issue of his salvation years before his death. He had been a Christ follower since I was in my late teens, and along the way we had enjoyed meaningful dialogue about the state of his soul.

For three years leading up to his death in December of 2005, my siblings, my mother, and I all believed that he would recover and live to see another fifteen or twenty years, but with every month that passed, we realized he was only getting worse. We eventually called in hospice services, and one night after I'd gone into a side room to take a nap, his body finally gave in. I was awakened just after 2:00 a.m. to learn that with only my loving mother at his side, Dad went to be with Jesus.

As I look back on that season of grief now, I realize that as soon as I knew my father was gone, I leaped into leadership mode. Throughout our lives, my older sister and younger brother had always looked to me for guidance during critical times, and so, operating out of sheer habit, I took the family reins in my grip, flinging myself fully into securing funeral home arrangements, ordering a casket, arranging the burial, organizing the memorial service, and so forth. In those moments, I was no longer the son. I was the reliable go-to guy who was making sure every last detail was effectively and efficiently tended to.

It was exactly how I behaved right after the shooting. Following both the loss of my dad and the loss of our innocence at New Life, I didn't take time until days later to fully and meaningfully grieve. And it's difficult to know how to move forward when you're not in touch with where you are.

After Christmas 2007 had come and gone, I headed to a friend's seven-thousand-acre ranch in southwest Arkansas to spend a few days alone, thinking, praying, and planning for the new year ahead. A country-folk haven positioned deep in the lush woods, it's one of my favorite places on earth. I arrived one afternoon, grabbed my Bible, hopped on a four-wheeler, and headed toward the banks of the Saline River — the same river I'd sat beside exactly one year prior, when God told me I'd be leaving Gateway Church.

"Please restore my soul," I asked God as I sat there this time. I asked him to help me make sense of all that had happened and to give me a supernatural infusion of his strength so that somehow I could go on. I didn't want to just get *through* the painful experience; I wanted to also draw *from* it what I needed to learn.

The opening words of Psalm 137 came to mind as I sat there that day. This psalm is thought to have been written toward the end of the Israelites' years spent in Babylonian captivity — an awful season when Hebrew homes had been taken from their rightful owners,

family members had been killed, the city of Jerusalem had been ran-
sacked, and able-bodied men, women, and children had been captured
as slaves. The psalmist mourns the plight of his countrymen, who
missed the way things used to be: "By the rivers of Babylon we sat and
wept when we remembered Zion" (v. 1). It's a simple sentence that
contains a boatload of weight.

I'm no therapist, but I think the three clear-cut ideas that show up
in this psalm are immensely useful in helping people work through
their pain. Disillusioned by all that had happened to them, the Israelites first came to grips with their new reality. They then wept for the
loss they'd suffered. And finally, they took time to remember the good
days that had passed.

Like me, you've probably heard stories about people who simply
can't deal with devastating loss. They stay firmly planted in one of
the first four stages of grief that we looked at earlier and absolutely
refuse to budge. For instance, a perfectly good bedroom in a home
goes unused because a grieving mother insists on leaving it just as it
was on the day her teenage daughter suddenly died. The mom's need
for a shrine overrides any semblance of good sense, and *denial* has its
way.

Or a young man returns from fighting in an overseas war and one
day fatally shoots a dozen strangers at a mall. The rage that has been
festering inside him for months finally finds its release in a random
act of violence—and *anger* stays put.

Or a thirtysomething woman pleads for the pregnancy she has
never known, promising God and anyone else listening that if that
one wish could somehow be granted, she'll be the best mom there
ever was. Refusing to invest time or energy in any other goal, she tries
to *bargain* her way into motherhood, the only role she believes can
satisfy her soul.

Or a small-business owner tallies his company's year-end numbers and realizes the economy is taking a tougher toll than even he
thought. Hours later the note left behind reveals that he just couldn't

find a way to go on. And *depression* adds another name to the list of those whose lives it has usurped.

In contrast to all these examples, the Israelites somehow found a way to keep putting one foot in front of the other, until they found themselves accepting and even thriving in their post-tragedy, post-sadness life. "By the rivers of Babylon we sat," verse 1 of Psalm 137 begins. No longer were they sitting beside the river of their beloved Jerusalem. *We're not in Israel any longer,* they reminded themselves. *Now we are bona fide slaves.*

"We live in different houses," they must have thought. "We occupy different jobs. We'll never see our loved ones again, until the day we reach heaven's door." They had to embrace a different reality and to admit that a new day had dawned.

But that was just step one. After the Hebrew people accepted their new reality, they then *stopped and wept over their loss.*

The worst advice I have ever heard doled out to someone struggling with the aftermath of great personal loss is this: "I know you're hurting, but the best thing you can do is get back to work. Don't let the pain have its way in your life; now's the time to stay busy and involved." Certainly, I understand the need to not wallow forever in grief. But the words of Psalm 137:1 should be instructive to us: at some point, you've got to stop and just cry.

After the shooting, there was a very real temptation for us as a church staff to keep our pain to a minimum and our busyness meters pegged. We needed to keep an entire church together; we needed all hands on deck — and *now.* But realistically, how well would that approach have served us? Stuffing the pain is a sorry strategy for success.

As I watched the easy flow of the Saline River on that late December afternoon, I felt a twinge of conviction inside. "You should probably slow down yourself, Brady," I thought. "Maybe cancel a few meetings next week." I knew that if I rushed back to Colorado, jumped full-bore into my jam-packed schedule, and forced myself to be productive even as my heart was still perplexed, I'd live to regret my decision and perhaps would never learn from the shooting what God was asking me to learn. Despite the demands tugging at my attention, I needed to give myself time to grieve. If the approach was good enough for God's chosen nation of Israel, then it was certainly good enough for me.

There was a third piece of advice I took away from Psalm 137:1 that day. In addition to accepting a new reality and giving themselves time and space to mourn, the Israelites also remembered Zion.

They remembered the temple where they once worshiped God.

They remembered the bustling city streets.

They remembered the markets where they once shopped.

They remembered the houses where they once lived.

They remembered the smell of the food they had cooked.

They remembered the peals of laughter as their kids had played with their friends.

As they sat beside the rivers of Babylon, a country utterly foreign to them, they remembered Zion, the beloved place they'd called home.

I thought about what it might look like to "remember Zion" in the context of the shooting, and God immediately brought an interesting idea to mind. I sensed him asking me to arrange a meeting between the Murray family and the Works family — the parents of the shooter and the parents of the ones who had been shot. *I want you to help them remember their Zion*, God seemed to say, *and to forge a path forward from here.*

It would be a critical step toward the vibrant future God had in store for us.

After returning home from Arkansas, I cleared my calendar for several days to allow myself space to mourn. Those hours spent beside the Saline River had been helpful, but I knew there was more soul-level work I needed to do. I tend to mourn in solitude, reading Scripture for hours on end. Some people journal their thoughts or dialogue with close friends; I just needed time and space to hear from God.

I also followed through on arranging the meeting between Loretta and Ron Murray and Marie and David Works. All four were godly people who seemed to be grieving well. But I wondered if meeting face-to-face would somehow ease the pain they felt.

First I called the Murrays. After exchanging preliminaries, I asked, "Would you be interested in coming to the campus so you can stand where your son lost his life?"

In response, they both exhaled audibly. "We weren't sure the request would be appropriate, coming from us," Loretta said. "But yes, we would love to do that. We would treasure seeing the exact location where Matthew spent his final moments here on earth."

Sensing their openness, I then asked if they might also like to meet Marie and David Works, the parents who had lost two daughters during the shooting. "We really would," came the reply.

After disconnecting the call, I immediately dialed one of New Life's pastors, Justin Spicer. I explained that I would be giving the Murrays a private tour of the campus and that as part of their visit, they had expressed interest in meeting David and his wife. "Would you mind calling David Works to see if he and Marie would be willing to join us for a meeting in my office?" I asked. I wanted to give David an out, in case nerves were still too raw for him and his wife to come. Having Pastor Justin place the call instead of me would hopefully remove any obligation to say yes.

As it turned out, David was in fact hesitant to agree to a meeting so soon. After all, it was coming on the heels of their family's first Christmas without Stephanie and Rachel. He requested a few days to talk to Marie and together to think about whether now was the right time. I knew that God had asked me to request the meeting; what happened from there was out of my hands. What's more, even if the Workses did agree to the meeting, I had no idea what would transpire. Would the interaction be volatile? Or would things veer toward the other end of the spectrum, yielding an uncomfortably silent room? There was only one way to find out.

Twenty-four hours after the invitation was extended, David Works called Pastor Justin and asked him to let me know that he and Marie were willing to attend the meeting. "I'm not sure how this all will go down," he said, "but we'll definitely come."

I hadn't let the media know of the meeting, and so on the cold and snowy morning of January 3, 2008—less than one month after the greatest tragedy our church had ever known—the perfect silence of New Life's foyer was pierced only by a quiet exchange between Ron and Loretta, a few of their family members, and me.

As we moved from the foyer to the children's ministry wing, I said, "Would you like me to give a chronological take on what happened on December 9?"

They both nodded slowly, as if to convince themselves their answer really was yes.

Sensing their trepidation, I stopped walking and asked, "Is there anything that you don't want to see or don't want to hear about?"

After a pause, the answer, they said, was no.

I felt sure that as the parents of the one who had caused utter mayhem for our church, they were unsure how to ask for precise detail about how the tragic events had actually unfolded. But I knew that now was the time to tell them the painful truth—and to show them as much of the shooting scene as they thought their hearts could bear.

I'd asked a few of New Life's pastors to join us for the walk-through, and after those men approached us, our larger but still-somber group made its way to the east parking lot first. Reaching the parking space where Matthew left his car, I retraced the route he had taken onto our campus and then explained where the Workses' van had been parked and pointed out where various shots had penetrated their vehicle.

We then moved inside the building, following the path Matthew had followed. I walked them up the hallway where he fired on our security guard, and then to the side hallway where he eventually died.

And as we stood at the spot where their son had passed away, the look on the Murrays' faces told me we had just stepped onto holy ground.

When a family suffers a tragic death, one of the ways to begin to find closure and to establish a sense of healing is to go to the place where that tragedy occurred. There is something significant about *place* — about the places where meaningful events happen to us. And as all of us stared down at the floor where Matthew had died, I heard waves of soft weeping. The other pastors and I wrapped loving arms around Loretta and Ron and prayed out loud that God would sustain them through their season of grief. We claimed God's forgiveness for all that had taken place on December 9, and we thanked him that even in the midst of tragedy, he was working all things together for good.

After that prayer, we were all silent for several minutes. Then, crouching down to touch the floor where Matthew had perished, Loretta Murray said, "Lord, what Satan came here to kill, I pray that you would bless."

It still gives me chills to consider that mom's heartfelt words. In that moment, it was as if something powerful was broken, something evil was foiled. Something that Satan had meant for great harm was being reclaimed for God's meaningful use.

Following what was a very difficult hour-long walk-through of the sights and events of December 9, I escorted Loretta and Ron Murray upstairs to my office, where the Works family was already waiting. As we neared the door, I wondered if this meeting was a good idea. The day had already been so emotional — would this exchange between the families help matters or make them worse?

I turned the handle on the door, entered my office ahead of the Murrays, greeted the Workses briefly, and then took several steps toward my corner desk. And what I witnessed in the moment that followed is something I won't ever forget. All four adults — Loretta and Ron Murray, Marie and David Works — embraced each other in a huddle and for many minutes did not let go.

Tears sprang to my eyes as I watched them clutch for each other, alternatively weeping and speaking out their heartfelt prayers. It was the most genuine display of forgiveness I have had the privilege of witnessing firsthand.

It went on this way for a full twenty minutes — the four of them crying, repenting, apologizing, forgiving, loving, praying, caring, ministering to each other. Eventually Ron Murray pulled back from the others' grip, looked at Marie and David Works, and through tear-clouded eyes said, "Please forgive us for what our son did."

Without a moment's hesitation David Works replied, "We are so sorry that you lost your son. . . ."

It was the beginning of the most powerful meeting of my entire ministry career, a meeting that would last for three hours before I would dismiss everyone in order to give their emotions a much-needed rest. For the majority of that session, I sat at my desk and watched from a distance as the two couples and their families gathered at my conference table and hashed through the events that had unexpectedly crossed their paths. I found it incredibly moving to see how God brought himself glory from the words that were exchanged.

After an hour or so, I noticed that the initial sweetness and energy of the room were giving way to sheer exhaustion. Not only had the dialogue that afternoon been difficult, but also I imagined both couples had spent an inordinate amount of energy in the days leading up to the meeting wondering exactly what would transpire once they arrived.

I got up from my desk, walked over to the table where they all sat, and said to the Murrays, "A couple of weeks ago, just before the memorial service for Marie and David's daughters Stephanie and Rachel, we all sat around and talked about happy memories from the girls' lives. It was helpful in the midst of our deep sadness to think back on better times, and I just wonder if we might do the same thing now, as it relates to Matthew.

"Listen, we all have heard a lot of bad news reports about your son in the month that has passed," I continued. "But he was once your little boy. You conceived him, you brought him home from the hospital, you celebrated his first steps and his birthdays and his every achievement along the way. For a few minutes here, would you mind sharing with the Works family and me a few fond memories you hold of your son? We would like to know Matthew Murray not as a young man who was struggling with severe issues and who came onto our campus to do great harm but as the boy you know and love."

It took Loretta and Ron no time at all to think of what to say. Immediately a flood of memories came out, of Matthew's love for soccer and his passion for putting together jigsaw puzzles in record time. They laughed as they recounted funny episodes that had punctuated his boyhood, and they teared up as they remembered sweet things he had said along the way. He was not a monster, as the media had painted him to be. He was this couple's beloved *son*, a child who had known great care and deep love.

The next Sunday, I stood in front of our entire congregation and recounted the meeting that had occurred. I closed my comments by saying, "If the Works family can choose to forgive in this manner, then we as a body must also forgive ... and then agree that it's time to move on." No sooner had the words come out of my mouth than the church erupted in applause. They were clearly ready to forgive.

Later that week, during a Wednesday morning all-staff meeting, I explained to my ministry colleagues how the whole deal had unfolded. I told them about sitting by the Saline River and hearing a clear prompting from God to initiate a healing conversation between the Workses and the Murrays. I walked them through the morning of January 3 — how the other pastors and I had shown Loretta and

Ron where their son tragically died—and then described the powerful meeting between the two families.

As I replayed the events from that week, I sensed a spirit of hopefulness flood the room. I told the staff about how God had brought to mind the words of Psalm 137 as I spent those days alone in Arkansas, and how I felt that in some small way, asking Loretta and Ron Murray to share their fond memories of their son, Matthew, led to a "remembering Zion" moment.

I told them I wanted the same thing for them.

"I'm still relatively new here," I said to the hundred or so staff members gathered with me. "But many of you have been here at New Life for twenty years or more. I want to clear the rest of this meeting's agenda and spend our time 'remembering Zion' instead."

I invited longtime staff to share their favorite memories of New Life, the place that hadn't always been known for scandal and shooting. I wanted to know what brought people to New Life, what they had enjoyed about their time on staff thus far, and the positive memories that had defined their time together.

One person told the story of how the church had been challenged one year to raise a certain amount of money for global missions, and if they hit the target, Pastor Ross Parsley would kiss a pig during that weekend's worship services. The congregation raised the goal amount and much more, and when the appointed weekend arrived, their beloved worship pastor puckered up to a small swine, right there on center stage.

Another staff member said that one weekend, nobody could find the anointing oil that is sometimes used during prayer times at the end of worship services. The culprit, it was later discovered, was one of Ted Haggard's kids, who had decided to fry up some lunch for himself in the church kitchen, using the anointing oil to coat the pan.

And then there was the story of how Pastor Ted unexpectedly announced during a Sunday night service that after his sermon there would be an ice cream and pie fellowship in the church atrium.

Unfortunately, his plan was also news to everyone else on his leadership team. Six or seven hundred congregants were now excitedly licking their lips over a dessert that simply did not exist.

In typical fashion, the ever-dependable Pastor Lance Coles sprang into action. While the evening service was still going on, he slipped out of the worship auditorium, headed to three different local grocery stores, bought as much ice cream and as many premade pies as he could fit in the trunk of his car, and raced back to New Life, where he would set up Ted's promised dessert.

By this point in our staff meeting, everyone was laughing so hard that they were crying. Various long-termers popped up from all over the room to tell of the times when hilarious mistakes were made, etiquette breaches were committed, well-meaning ministry went awry, and more. The conversation was so robust that we wound up devoting not one but two weekly staff meetings to hearing people's tales. It was a fantastic time of connection for us all.

It is said that laughter is good for the bones (Prov. 17:22), and after those two meetings, my belief in that proverb was refreshed. I would later hear from members of our staff that the sessions had been cathartic for them. "It matters to us that you care about our past," one person said. "This place holds wonderful memories too."

Indeed it does.

Regardless of the pain we as a body have endured, we must always remember our Zion, the days when profound peace prevailed. Yes, we had been forced to enter a new reality, and we had been given cause to sit and weep. But as we devoted ourselves to acknowledging the good that God had done in our midst, our faith was strengthened. At least for a while.

Several months after those life-giving staff meetings, things would take a turn for the worse. Further allegations of moral misconduct regarding Ted Haggard surfaced, and the momentum that we as a church were finally building seemed to dissipate into thin air. For weeks on end, I wrestled with my calling at New Life and believed my joy was gone for good. Many people in our congregation were still struggling with the aftermath of the shooting; many more wondered if their own church had orchestrated a series of payoffs to other people who claimed they had been harmed by Ted (in fact, we had not); the national economy was tanking, which took a terrible toll among our congregation — on business owners and employees alike; and three hundred to four hundred people chose to leave New Life and start their own church a few miles away. Everywhere I looked, I saw storm clouds forming. These were difficult days.

About that time, Jimmy Evans — my pastor friend from west Texas who was well aware that I was experiencing a challenging season — called and asked if we could talk. In the midst of such a tumultuous turn of events, his kind and caring voice immediately put me at ease.

He asked if I'd seen the national weather reports lately and said that his part of the country had been experiencing a series of strong storms — lightning, wind, hail, the whole deal. "But we'll take whatever rain we can get," he said.

He reminded me how dry the climate is in west Texas and said that sometimes the only moisture they get in Amarillo is from those violent thunderstorms that threaten to do them in. He then suggested to me that while all I could see was the lightning, the wind, and the hail all around — the swirl of trouble that seemed to have our church in its grip — there was also some necessary rain in the storm we were enduring. It was good rain. It was *helpful* rain. It was moisture we all desperately needed.

I was taken back to the little chat I'd had with God before I accepted the role at New Life. As I mentioned, Pam and I had flown to Colorado Springs so I could interview for the job, and as I sat in our hotel room on the last morning of our stay, God had asked me if I would be willing not to plant a church but to water one that was unquestionably parched.

God was watering something at New Life, and the last thing I wanted to do was miss out on whatever that was. I love a slow, steady rain as much as the next person, but thanks to a single phone call from a prophetic friend whose voice I deeply value, I was reminded that life doesn't always work like that. Sometimes it takes a massive band of storms to bring the nourishing rain that's required.

Two weeks after that timely phone call from Jimmy Evans, Dr. Ken Ulmer flew from his home church on the south side of Los Angeles to New Life Church to speak during our weekend services. Several months prior, Dr. Ulmer had been named the president of King's College and Seminary, and around that same time his predecessor, Dr. Jack Hayford, had graciously introduced us.

I had no idea what topic Dr. Ulmer planned to preach on when he stepped onto the platform during the morning's first worship service, but five minutes into the meat of his talk, I knew we were in for a divine feast. Leaning into Solomon's prayer of dedication over God's temple, recorded in 2 Chronicles 6, Dr. Ulmer said, "Just as Solomon asked his heavenly Father to show the worshipers who had gathered in that temple the right way to live, and to send rain on the land he had given his people as an inheritance, I pray that God will pour out on *this* house a special anointing for the prayers of the people who will gather."

"Hear me, New Life Church," he continued. "I pray one word for you: *rain.*"

I had not had a single conversation with Dr. Ulmer about the state of affairs of my heart. He knew nothing about the drought I felt we were enduring as a church and about Jimmy Evans's prophecy of rain. And yet rain is what he preached about, a supernatural watering that would beautifully bless our lives. Coincidence? I strongly doubted that.

Evidently, I can be hardheaded, because God sent still a third emissary my way in an attempt to convince me that he was still on the throne, that I was still called to serve at New Life, and that the storm clouds which had surrounded me would eventually pass on by.

A few weeks after Dr. Ulmer's fantastic talk, and following our early Sunday morning worship service one weekend, a man from the congregation sent me a message with what he believed was a word from God.

"Brady," his note began, "I was watching you speak this morning, and partway through your sermon, I was kind of caught away by God. He kept whispering the word *diminishment* to me and compelling me to pray against any power that feelings of diminishment might have in your life."

My initial reaction as I read the man's words was, "Huh? Me? Diminished?" The guy obviously didn't know me well. I am a self-confident person, and while I've dealt with my share of insecurity along the way, "diminished" isn't exactly how I'd describe myself now.

"I pray today against diminishment in your life," the man's closing words read. And with that, he just signed off.

As I closed and deleted the email, I was tempted to dismiss the input altogether. But days later I found myself still fixated on that word. "*Diminishment.* What am I supposed to glean from *diminishment?*" I wondered. I dug around a bit to try to uncover every possible meaning of the word, and what I'd soon discover would rock my world.

To be diminished is to have your authority, dignity, or reputation lessened. It is to forfeit your God-given influence by focusing on all that is wrong. For example, when I arrived at New Life, the building was in dire need of new carpet, new tile flooring, new paint, and new signage, both inside and out. Over a several-month period of time, we had raised enough money — by inviting the congregation to participate in a special "home improvement" offering — that new carpet had been rolled out, new tile had been laid, and fresh coats of paint now covered nearly every wall. Additionally, we'd added huge new high-definition screens inside the Living Room to aid everyone's worship experience by making song lyrics and Scripture passages easier to read and the speaker easier to see.

But we still hadn't replaced those signs.

I'd walk through our building each day and see drab blue signs hanging from the ceiling or plastered on the wall and think, "This building is in such terrible shape. We've got to do something about those signs."

I'd look right past the positive and focus only on what was still wrong. This is what is called diminishment, and I was falling prey to it left and right.

Especially after crisis and great pain, it's common to battle diminishment, to fixate on the grave illness, the troubling financial reality, the untimely death, the prodigal nature of the child, the horrors of all that has happened, and the bleakness of the scene all around. We lose sight of the beautiful things God is accomplishing, of the good he is determined to do.

I thought about Jimmy's prophetic word and about the rain-filled blessing Dr. Ulmer had declared over our church, and before God I resolved that I would not fixate on the storm. Instead, I would choose to see the rain for what it was — moisture we desperately needed, a cleansing that would help us to heal. I pictured Andy Dufresne, the main character in the movie *The Shawshank Redemption*, bursting out of the half-mile sewage-tunnel system that led the innocent escapee from Shawshank State Prison to freedom, ripping off his standard-issue shirt, throwing his weary arms into the air, and thrusting his face skyward as he soaked up the pouring rain, and I thought with newfound appreciation, "God, thank you for this storm."

New Life Church would be defined neither by scandal and shooting nor by the wind, the hail, and the lightning we had endured. We would be defined instead by the remnants of much-needed *rain* — by refreshment and renewal that can come only from heaven above.

* * *

Isaiah 61:2–3 offers a series of promises to those who mourned in ancient times—and to you and me when we grieve today. Speaking prophetically of Jesus Christ, this passage says that a major reason why the Messiah would come in human flesh to planet Earth was to "comfort all who mourn." He would "bestow on them a crown of beauty instead of ashes, the oil of gladness instead of mourning, and a garment of praise instead of a spirit of despair."

I can't pinpoint the exact date or time when the shift occurred, but somewhere along the way—during the eighteen months it took to move from the lion exhibit to the giraffes—beauty really did spring up from ashes. Gladness really did take mourning's place. And the despair I had come to believe would never depart morphed somehow into heartfelt praise. I woke up one day in June 2009 and realized I was available for God's use once more.

Let me explain what I mean.

Scores of people I know have suffered great loss in life and are emotionally shut down as a result. They never learned to properly mourn and grieve, and so the pain gets stuffed farther down. The day finally dawns when they can't engage in any aspect of life because their enthusiasm and passion are gone. They can't engage with their spouse. They can't engage with their kids. They can't engage with their role at work. They can't engage with the vision for their local church. The emotional toll they've been carrying prohibits them from engaging in *any* aspect of life. And as a result, they are unavailable to God and others to be salt and light in the world.

I saw this play out firsthand at New Life. A couple who have faithfully served our body for many years approached me one weekend and said, "Brady, we love what God is doing among this church and how you are leading us into a brighter future, but for some reason we just stay stuck. We haven't been able to get involved like we used to be involved. We haven't been able to worship like we used to worship. We aren't serving like we used to serve."

Without intending to, this couple had allowed themselves to

become unavailable to God. They had neglected to adequately mourn the losses they had suffered, and spiritually and physically they couldn't find their way back to full engagement.

As you and I learn to grieve properly — and fully — we see God show up with comfort for our weary souls. The two actions move back and forth in waves: we grieve, God comforts, we grieve, God comforts even more. He exchanges our ashes for beauty and gives gladness where mourning once was. Our growth — a "planting of the LORD," as the prophet Isaiah put it (Isa. 61:3) — displays God's splendor. *This is why I equip you to eventually move on from pain*, God essentially says, *so that my glory can be gathered through you.*

Months after the shooting, we as a church broke ground, laid soil, and planted two tall, beautiful blue spruce trees of remembrance on the parking spot where Stephanie and Rachel Works had been shot. And on that crisp weekday morning, God's promise was on our minds. What Satan meant for death would bring forth undeniable life. Where a spirit of despair had once clouded our sight, pure praise would be on our lips. We declared that we were ready to move forward, to pursue whatever kingdom dreams God had on his mind. Our time with the lions was over; a new exhibit was calling our name.

Long after that coffee meeting with the dad who encouraged me to lead our congregation to the next exhibit, God finally revealed to me more detail about where we were to move on to as a church. One of our worship leaders, Jon Egan, had recently written a song titled "Light Up the World," the lyrics of which are based on a life verse of mine, James 1:27, which says, "Religion that God our Father accepts as pure and faultless is this: to look after orphans and widows in their distress and to keep oneself from being polluted by the world." Through his powerful song, Jon was encouraging the church to be the hands and feet of Christ, to return to her ancient roots, and to rise up in this generation to make a difference for good and for God.

Weeks prior, our church had challenged students in our high school ministry to raise funds to build two orphanages in Uganda, and not surprising to me, they raised enough to build four. When the orphanages were set to open, Jon and a film crew flew to Africa to document the Ugandan children moving into their new home. Much of the footage they captured would wind up in a music video for the song.

I was sitting in my home office tending to a few emails when Jon's YouTube link floated in. "Check out what I just posted," his message to me read. "It's for 'Light Up the World.'"

Those who know me best would confirm that I'm not a very emotional guy. But as I sat there in front of my laptop that night, tears of joy streamed shamelessly down my cheeks. God was directing me toward our next exhibit, courtesy of a single verse I have loved for years. *I'm asking you to care for the widows and orphans in your midst,* I sensed God saying to me. *And to take whatever steps you must take in order to keep your heart as a leader pure.*

The details of that vision would take time to work out, but instantly I was infused with hope. The God who had promised never to leave or forsake us had proven himself faithful once more. He would comfort us and transform us.

He would gently guide us toward those giraffes.

PART 3

CHOOSING TO OVERCOME

As we at New Life began to move from the darkness
of the valley to the mountaintop waiting on the other side,
we noticed a beneficial byproduct
of the suffering we had endured:
what Satan had meant for our undoing,
God was using for good.
The opposition that had taunted us, terrified us,
and threatened to take us out
was no match for the work
God was determined to accomplish in our midst.

Redemption,
Repentance, and Other
Purposes of Pain

God does not always heal us instantly the way we think.
He is not a jack-in-the-box God.
But God is walking with me through this.
— *Thelma Wells*

EARLY IN MY TENURE AT NEW LIFE CHURCH, I CROSSED PATHS WITH Jim Daly, president and CEO of Focus on the Family, a Christian ministry committed to helping families thrive. Almost instantly I knew we'd be friends. Many months after that initial introduction, Jim and I were grabbing lunch one day at P. F. Chang's. I don't recall how we got on the subject, but seemingly out of the blue, Jim said, "Brady, did you know that there are only about eight hundred orphans in the entire state of Colorado?"

My ears immediately perked up. God had been prompting me toward living out the James 1:27 reminder that pure and faultless religion, according to God, would *always* involve caring for people in distress—both old and young. Evidently, he was laying similar themes in the heart of Jim, who grew up in the foster care system in Long

Beach, California, after his mother died, his stepfather walked out, and he and his siblings were all but left to fend for themselves.

As I mentioned earlier, when we lived in Texas, my wife and I adopted two kids who may have had an equally tough life had we not invited them into our family. Thankfully, not only did Jim and I both understand how it felt to be adopted in the ultimate sense of the word —that is, to be intentionally placed in the family of God—but also we knew the power of providing a loving Christian home for children as a means of introducing them to that God.

"There are more than forty thousand orphans in Los Angeles County and Orange County alone," Jim continued, his forkful of kung pao chicken suspended in midair, "and yet in our entire *state*, there are less than eight hundred."

He let the comment hang between us for a moment before saying anything else, but I knew exactly where he was going.

"There are about three thousand Bible-believing churches in Colorado," he added.

Picking up on his train of thought, I said, "If we challenged each church to adopt just one boy or girl from the state system, we'd need only, what, about a quarter of the churches to say yes in order to place every orphaned kid in Colorado in a loving home?"

Jim nodded.

In fact, in this country in a given year, there are 135,000 kids waiting to find families who will take them in, and more than 300,000 churches in the United States. If even *every other* church got on board by saying yes to just one child, we would have this problem solved.

Suffice it to say, the end result of that lunchtime conversation was a joint effort between New Life and Focus on the Family, along with hundreds of other churches throughout our area who are also committed to making Colorado the first state in the Union to have a waiting list of parents who want to adopt children, instead of a list of kids waiting for somebody to rescue them someday.

The first informational meeting that we held at New Life for people interested in learning about the Wait No More initiative yielded the largest single gathering of prospective adoptive parents ever assembled in the United States, about fifteen hundred adults. We were blown away. The energy and enthusiasm in the room boosted our collective spirit in ways we hadn't seen for many months. Finally, our attention was shifting from devastation and tragedy to a new thing God was doing in our midst. This was the "next exhibit" we had been craving, the long-awaited mission we sought. For the first time since the shooting, we had a goal in mind that had nothing to do with recovery and *everything* to do with charging ahead for the kingdom of God. We wanted God to stir adults' hearts. We wanted to see kids placed in Christian families. And we wanted to end the trend of orphans having no consistent place to call home.

My assistant, Karla, and her husband, Brandon, were among the New Life families who took in a child, and as I watched them walk through the process of rescuing four-year-old Alisa from a dysfunctional environment, my heart swelled. Once all the paperwork had been filed and the judge's gavel had come down in favor of Alisa officially becoming Karla and Brandon's daughter, our entire church family celebrated by dedicating her to Jesus Christ that weekend.

On that Sunday morning during the eleven o'clock worship service, I called Karla, Brandon, and Alisa up to the stage — along with their extended family and close friends — and we prayed a prayer of blessing over little Alisa's life. I glanced down at her during that prayer and for the first time saw utter delight sweep over her face. She was looking out at the thousands of New Lifers who were standing in solidarity to say before God and before each other that they were committing themselves to giving Alisa every possible resource so she could grow up safe, secure, and well loved. Even at four years old, she seemed to catch the importance of what was happening that day.

It has been nearly eighteen months since we held that initial informational meeting on our campus, and so far, more than 500 boys and girls have been adopted into loving, Christian families, both at

New Life and around the state. I expect that in the next year and a half, the other 350 will be placed. It's the church at her finest, in my view. While there must always be a reliable governmental system for protecting unparented children from harm, the church ought to be waiting outside the state's secure doors, ready to receive those kids with outstretched arms. After all, adoption is inherent to the core of the Christian faith. The gospel message is *centered* on the theme of adoption, for God chose us as sons and daughters, pulling us out of the orphanage called the world and placing us into his forever family, a community established by love and faith.

As those of us at New Life have watched one child after another be enfolded by caring, Christ-following moms and dads, our belief that God is restoring all that we lost has been renewed. Granted, nothing will ever undo the pain that the shooting caused. Moreover, nothing will ever bring back Rachel and Stephanie Works. But having dozens of children join our church family in the months following the Works girls' deaths showed us in a tangible way that God really does turn even our deepest grief into joy. He was redeeming our situation, as awful as it was.

Galatians 4 contains an important summary of how this marvelous thing called redemption works. Beginning in verse 1, we read this:

> I mean that the heir, as long as he is a child, is no different from a slave, though he is the owner of everything, but he is under guardians and managers until the date set by his father. In the same way we also, when we were children, were enslaved to the elementary principles of the world. But when the fullness of time had come, God sent forth his Son, born of woman, born under the law, to redeem those who were under the law, so that we might receive adoption as sons. And because you are sons, God has sent the Spirit of his Son into our hearts, crying, "Abba! Father!" So

you are no longer a slave, but a son, and if a son, then an heir
through God.
                                        —*Galatians 4:1–7 ESV*

As that passage reminds us, you and I once were slaves to our sin,
to our rebellion, to the useless principles of this world. And because of
our inability to meet the standard set by the law we were to obey, we
deserved absolutely nothing more than *justice*. Somebody needed to
pay for the wrongdoing we had done, but we were incapable of cover-
ing the massive debt we'd incurred. Seeing our hopeless situation for
what it was, we decided the best we could do was to beg for mercy:
"God, please take pity on me just this one time!"

But then, miraculously, in the instantaneous humbling of our
hearts before God, we were given something far greater than mercy;
in that moment, we were gifted instead with *grace*. We weren't given
justice, which is getting exactly what we deserve. Nor were we merely
given mercy, which is *not* getting what we deserve. But we were given
grace, in effect *getting* what we *absolutely did not deserve*. We saw our
shortcomings and begged for mercy, but grace is what we got. God's
ultimate riches. A place in heaven. And adoption into his family even
now, while we're on earth.

This is what redemption is all about.

In Western culture, when we say something sounds too good to be
true, it probably *is* too good to be true. This concept of getting grace
when justice is what we deserve definitely fits that bill. If you're like
me, you grew up learning that if you want to get ahead in this world,
you have to roll up your sleeves, put in your time, and pull yourself up
by your bootstraps when you fall down. To a certain extent, I agree
with that. As Christ's followers, we *should* be the ones showing up
early, working harder than anyone else, leading the way as much as
we can. But at the end of all those worthy efforts, we must understand
that nothing we have done is able to secure the salvation we seek.
Works are important, but they do not determine eternal destination.

For our eternal destination is determined not by works but solely by what we *believe*.

Think of it this way: if we could do enough good to get to heaven, then there was no reason for Jesus to come to planet Earth and die. In fact, the "goodness" of humankind was not good enough to earn favor with God. Sin still existed, which meant separation from him still existed too. It is for this reason that Jesus Christ left heaven, lived a blameless life on earth, endured a torturous death, and rose as our resurrected Messiah on the third day. He did all those things so we could be saved—so *redemption* could be ours.

Typically, when I explain this idea to people whose paths I happen to cross, I get one of two reactions. One group of people looks at me with a countenance that seems to say, "I totally agree with you. And although I am a good person who doesn't really need all this grace stuff, I'm sure glad you're out there spreading this message for the bad people who are wrecking our world." That group believes they are somehow above grace, that they are above salvation, that they are above the need for redemption, thanks to their picture-perfect lives.

For what it's worth, they are not.

And then there is group two. Group two is made up of "bad" people who wish they were part of the "good" group only so they wouldn't be in need of grace. It's a mistaken assumption at its core, because even the *best* people desperately need grace. Everybody— regardless of background, race, religion, and socioeconomic status —needs grace. If the worse sin you ever committed was flushing a goldfish down the commode, you—yes, even you—are in need of grace. You and I both need grace in order to be made right with God, no matter who we are or what we have done. We need God's redeeming ways to take effect in our lives so we can be returned to the original plan he had in store for our lives when he knit us together before we were born.

* * *

The word around New Life for many months following the double-whammy challenge of a scandal and a deadly shooting on our campus was that by all measures, our church should have been shut down and our property turned into a used-car lot. And frankly, on some days I thought the jokesters had it about right. What church survives the kind of scandal and violence we'd endured? What church recovers all that has been lost when that loss seems so unbelievably great? It was far easier for me to believe that we'd spiral downward into becoming nothing more than a pile of ugly rubble than to buy into the idea that a bright future lay ahead. But during those darker moments, my thoughts eventually would chase back to the words of Isaiah 61 that God had laid on my heart before.

"I'll give you beauty in exchange for those ashes," those verses read. "The oil of gladness instead of mourning. A garment of praise instead of a spirit of despair." God was reminding me that despite how we felt in our hearts, the people of New Life would somehow become sturdy and strong once again.

Later in that same chapter of the Bible, it says that even after terrible devastation, God will reward his people for their suffering. Isn't that an amazing promise? "Instead of their shame," verse 7 says, "my people will receive a double portion, and instead of disgrace they will rejoice in their inheritance; and so they will inherit a double portion in their land, and everlasting joy will be theirs."

A double portion instead of disgrace? Was God *sure* about a promise like that? Something in me knew that the answer was yes for our church—and it remains yes for your life too.

I have a theory about the purpose of suffering in our lives, and it's that every struggle that you and I face along the way is an opportunity to experience the redemption of God. It is clear from Scripture that because our enemy is so crafty at tripping us up, we must lean into the power of God. Surely, you have seen this dynamic at work in your own life, as I have so often in mine: if I were stronger than the enemy who works to ruin my life, I'd depend very little on God. If I had the ability within myself to defeat Satan and his evil schemes, then I would go on about my daily life with hardly a glance toward God. Simply put, it is *because* I cannot defeat Satan in my own strength that I live in complete surrender to God. And each time my heavenly Father rescues me from one of Satan's snares, I watch with fresh appreciation as redemption has its marvelous way.

And so it was that as we at New Life began to move from the darkness of the valley to the mountaintop waiting on the other side, we noticed a beneficial byproduct of the suffering we had endured: what Satan had meant for our undoing, God was using for good. The opposition that had taunted us, terrified us, and threatened to take us out was no match for the work God was determined to accomplish in our midst.

There were perhaps dozens of manifestations of what I'm talking about, but let me give you just the top four. As God went about his restorative ways, the first thing we saw him redeem was our unity as a church. As with any group of imperfect people, there were small factions that had gone unchecked at New Life. But as soon as a group is forced to face a life-and-death situation together, those divisions often dissipate into thin air. It really is true that you can't defend somebody you're choosing to be offended by. For us to attain victory over the suffering we had endured meant we needed to band together as one.

A second object of God's redemption was our collective depth of faith. When life is coasting along and everything seems breezy and bright, it's easy to become casual with what you believe. But when you see an enemy come barging through the door of your life, guns drawn, steps sure, rage-fueled expression set, you either dissolve into a puddle of fear or decide to get serious about your faith. As a result of enduring intense suffering, our church began to pray with greater intensity, read the Bible with greater consistency, and love with greater selflessness than we'd ever manifested before.

I don't covet the means that it took, but what a fantastic end!

The third object of God's redemption was our vigilance. Coming face-to-face with a vicious enemy causes you to live in a more circumspect manner. As a result, as a church we were forced to tread more carefully along life's path. First Peter 5:8 says that as Christ's followers, we are to be "self-controlled and alert" because our enemy "prowls around like a roaring lion looking for someone to devour." I don't know about you, but if I found myself alone on the plains of Africa and saw a hungry lion appear, I'd do everything in my power to stay concealed from his direct line of sight. The metaphor isn't too far removed from how we behave at New Life these days.

I'm convinced that Satan would still love to see our church fail. As a result, I evaluate situations more carefully. I make decisions more soberly. I try to use words more wisely. I refuse to cave to timidity, but I reject signing up to be lion bait as well.

Lastly, as we saw God's redemptive plan unfold all around us, we noticed that the one thing we felt had been stolen from us was slowly starting to reemerge: our innocence.

In Mark 10:15, Jesus is quoted as saying, "I tell you the truth, anyone who will not receive the kingdom of God like a little child will never enter it." Interestingly, as Jesus spoke those words, he did so with a bunch of little kids on his lap. The text says that people from the surrounding areas were bringing their children to Jesus so he could bless them, but the disciples thought it was a waste of their master's time. They rebuked the parents, and Jesus in turn rebuked *them*. "Let the little children come to me," Jesus asserted, "and do not hinder them, for the kingdom of God belongs to such as these" (Mark 10:14). Then he gathered the children into his arms, put his hands on them, and *blessed* them.

I'd like to make an observation here. Unlike their grown-up counterparts, children are *always* ready to receive a gift. Always. If there are kids in your life, then try this experiment today: offer those miniature people something in exchange for nothing, and just see what they do.

I'll tell you what they'll do. They will take the gift! They may not stop to say thank you, but I assure you they will take the gift.

Contrast that with how adults behave when offered something for free. Certainly, there are exceptions, but many adults feel a wave of guilt sweep over them when they are forced to simply *receive* with open hands. But this is exactly the posture God would have us hold, where his kingdom is concerned.

Last February, a giant box appeared on our doorstep, addressed to my kids. Without even glancing at the return address, I knew exactly who it was from: the grandparents. Valentine's Day was less than a week away, which meant yet one more excuse to lavish my children with gifts.

As Callie and her brother tore into the goods, she looked up at me with dancing eyes and said, "Dad! We hit the jackpocket!"

I thought about correcting her — "It's jack*pot*, Callie" — but I knew her attention was elsewhere and wasn't returning anytime soon.

A few weeks ago they hit the "jackpocket" again as Easter neared. Another box on the doorstep, another ten minutes of parental harassment, *two* sets of eyes dancing. "Can we open it, Dad? How about now? Pleeease? Can we open it *now*?" And as the fake Easter grass covered every possible surface in our house, I thought, "This is exactly how God wants us to be." He wants us to behave in his presence like children, who *receive* with open and thankful hearts.

The first sentence Jesus uttered in the greatest sermon ever preached is this: "Blessed are the poor in spirit, for theirs is the kingdom of heaven" (Matt. 5:3). In his day, there were two types of poor people, the *professional poor*, who had learned to survive by working the system as beggars, and the *desperate poor*, those who because of sickness or an accident had become poor and, barring consistent help from kind passersby, were most likely going to die.

It was the desperate ones to whom Jesus was speaking. The desperate poor weren't looking to swindle the system. They knew exactly how hopeless they were and had only one option left to them, which was to humbly *receive* with open hands. They could only become like little children, totally needy before God each day.

This same sense of honest desperation enveloped our church over time. Every illusion of earning our way into God's favor had been banished; unmerited redemption is what we now sought. And what has been true for us is true for you too: regardless of what needs to be redeemed in your life, I hope you know God stands ready to restore whatever has been lost.

I meet countless believers in God who are not living with power in the present because they can't let go of a shameful past. Maybe you can't grasp the idea that God would forgive you for all you've done. Sure, you believe that you're born again and that you have been miraculously saved. You just can't talk yourself into believing that your past really has been erased.

As a result, you forge ahead with good works on your mind, trying to earn divine favor with God.

If what I'm describing is true of you, I hope you'll recall the words of Romans 8:1 – 2. It says, "There is now no condemnation for those who are in Christ Jesus, because through Christ Jesus the law of the Spirit of life set me free from the law of sin and death."

Did you catch that opening phrase? There is now *no* condemnation, if you are in Christ Jesus. It doesn't say that we receive a little bit of condemnation, maybe a smidgen if we've been *really* bad. It says we get no condemnation, zero condemnation — zilch, nada, *none*.

Later in that same chapter, verses 38 – 39 say this: "I am convinced that neither death nor life, neither angels nor demons, neither the present nor the future, nor any powers, neither height nor depth, nor anything else in all creation, will be able to separate us from the love of God that is in Christ Jesus our Lord."

If there is one goal I have in writing this chapter, it's that you would come away utterly convinced that you are loved and accepted and redeemed. Despite the pain, despite the suffering, despite the disappointment and grief you've known, your heavenly Father *loves* you and is committed to redeeming what was lost. Remember your redemption! Fix your attention on the truth that nothing can remove you from God's care.

Not death.

Not life.

Not angels.

Not demons.

Not anything that happens today.

Not anything that may happen tomorrow.

Not any power.

Not any height or depth or anything else in all of creation.

Nothing can separate you from God.

No condemnation.

No separation.

Nothing but redemption and grace.

Isn't that a better way to live life? Just imagine how much security and freedom believers all over the world would realize if only they would let go of the fear of being condemned or being unloved. Chains of bondage would fall away instantly as God's people rose up and declared that Satan's schemes have no chance when pitted against our Father's redemptive ways.

When you and I opt to live in light of God's love, acceptance, and redemption, we accept with open hands the work Jesus accomplished on our behalf on the cross. So that grace could be extended to you and me, God sent the purest of lambs, Jesus Christ, to suffer and to die. We were the ones with the debt to pay, but he willingly covered it instead. And when we allow redemption to have its way in our lives, we exchange sentences with Christ. We trade our debt for his payment; we trade our punishment for his reward.

You may remember the story of the two thieves who found themselves hanging next to Jesus after he was nailed to the cross. The humble thief had been tried, found guilty, and sentenced to a gruesome death. There he was, waiting for his crucifixion to steal his very last breath, when he realized that he was beside the Redeemer of all humankind.

He had nothing to offer God at that point. What was he going to do, hop down off his cross for a few minutes so he could go find everyone he had stolen from and apologize for ripping them off? He also couldn't walk an aisle, step into a baptistery, or check off a few good deeds. All he could do was make a simple request and see what Jesus would do: "Jesus," he said, "remember me when you come into your kingdom" (Luke 23:42).

In reply, he got more than justice or mercy; he received astounding, amazing grace. Jesus answered, "I tell you the truth, today you will be with me in paradise" (v. 43).

Jesus didn't offer the man paradise because of his laudable works. He offered it simply because a sin-scarred human being was willing to finally be redeemed. *That* is what it looks like to let pain birth something good.

But that's not the end of the story. There's still a role you and I must play.

I was driving down the interstate a few days ago and noticed a billboard advertising the current estimated Powerball winnings in Colorado Springs. Evidently, the total stood at 120 trillion dollars or something; the zeroes went clear off the sign. It occurred to me as I drove past that sign that not being willing to repent of your sinful ways to turn toward God's redemption is akin to refusing to cash in the winning Powerball ticket. Instead, you slip that ticket into your back pocket, thinking, "I'll just hang on to this for a while." That turning toward redemption is also what we call repentance, and it is the necessary precursor to receiving the grace of God.

The word *repentance* comes from two Greek words that mean to change your mind or change your direction. Suppose a man you know is whittling away what's left of his life worshiping himself instead of

God. He spends every waking hour trying to find a way to accumulate more stuff, believing that material possessions somehow will satisfy his soul. His time, his talents, his money, his *life*—everything revolves around him. But then a buddy of his tells him about grace, and he realizes he's been getting it all wrong. "I made for a terrible god!" he says to himself, as he decides to go God's way instead.

He turns from his selfishness, he surrenders his life to Jesus Christ, and he allows God's will for his life to unfold. Soon he comes to understand that the fulfillment he tried to gain by worshiping himself could be found only in God.

What he has experienced is repentance—arresting movement in one direction and then going a new way with your life. Interestingly, somewhere between 80 percent and 90 percent of people in the United States claim they are Christians, and yet I wonder how many of those men and women have done the work that repentance requires. Mark 1:15 quotes Jesus as saying we must both repent *and* believe if we want to be considered followers of his.

That verse comes immediately after John the Baptist, known as a renegade for baptizing new believers in the name of Jesus Christ, is imprisoned. Mark 1:14 says, "After John was put in prison, Jesus went into Galilee, proclaiming the good news of God." It was news of God's grace that he was spreading, which for that audience must have seemed too good to be true, as it still seems to us today.

Jesus' audience probably wondered what they had to do to garner God's favor and spend eternity with him. But Jesus' response surely surprised them. "Repent and believe," he said. "That's it—repent and believe." The only two things that were required for grace were simply to repent and believe. It was true two-thousand-plus years ago, and it remains true for us here and now.

So how do you know if you have actually repented, if you have positioned yourself for God's power to course its way through your life, redeeming the pain? First John 2:3 would answer the question this way: if you have actually come to know God by receiving his gift of grace, then one thing will be true of your life—you will *choose to obey his commands.* In other words, the ones who say, "I know God," but refuse to do what God asks them to do are liars, according to the Bible. That is, the truth is not present in them.

Now, if you know someone like this, my advice is not to lead off your next conversation by calling them a liar. Let that revelation come to them from God instead of from you. But if the someone we're talking about happens to be *you,* then I suggest you take action immediately so you can begin to walk in the truth.

This may rock your theology, but people do not go to hell because of sin. People go to hell because of *unbelief.* The Bible says that when Jesus hung on the cross more than two thousand years ago, just before he died he said three very important words: "It is finished" (John 19:30). All the sins that humanity had committed previously, all the sins committed over the subsequent two thousand years since the cross, and all the sins of tomorrow were paid for with one death and one resurrection of Jesus. He cannot and will not go back to the cross; it stands to reason, then, that if he will never return to the cross, he must have paid for 100 percent of sin right then and there, for all time.

I'll say it again: the reason why people go to hell has nothing to do with their sin. Instead, it has everything to do with whether or not they believe in Jesus Christ as the only sacrifice sufficient to wash those shortcomings away. I've often told New Lifers that the torment of hell will not be some sort of suspension in utter darkness, where people think about their sins all day. The torment of hell will be sitting in that darkness with the realization that all they had to do in order to live in eternal light was take the all-too-simple step of *choosing to believe.*

Repent and believe. Turn toward redemption and believe that God is ready to provide it. That's all it takes to see beauty emerge from the ashes you hold in this life.

* * *

As I've said, times of deep brokenness allow us to see the redemptive power of God at work in living color. But those times of brokenness also provide fantastic opportunities for us to fix what is ours alone to fix.

Once we as a church mopped up the tears we had shed over all we had lost, it was as if a mirror were held up to our collective face, showing us the broken places that weren't God's — but ours — to repair. Where had we lost heart along the way? In what ways did our priorities need to shift? What agreements were we making with things not born of God — diminishment, hopelessness, pain?

We knew that our loving heavenly Father was in the process of redeeming what had been taken from us, but in the meantime we decided to use our divinely given gifts, talents, and energies to fix what we had the power to fix. For starters, we shifted our priority as a staff to being more missional in our mindset and not taking such an "attractional" approach, where everything centered on gearing up for and successfully executing the next big event. As a first step in this new direction, I sent our key leaders away in staggered fashion for six-week sabbaticals, so they could return to the ideas of rest, of replenishment, of diligently seeking God's face. Upon their return, we all submitted ourselves to greater personal and professional accountability so we wouldn't burn out again, as many of them had after losing their pastor.

Together, with repentant hearts, we were saying, "God, we don't understand all that has unfolded around here, but we refuse to be shaken from the foundation you placed us on years ago. We insist on clinging to you and to your will. Above anything else, we are lovers of God. That is who we are today and who we forever hope to be."

At its core, repentance is not merely emotional; it must be plainly actionable too. It is not just expressing remorse; it is also embracing a new way of life. And so, as a staff and as a church, we decided that we'd never know God's full redemption until we stopped heading in errant directions and allowed his leadership in our lives.

Author and Bible teacher John MacArthur says that in terms of this redemption/repentance equation, "what is required of God is to provide atonement and secure the sinner," and "what is required of the man or the woman is to repent and believe.... That is the sum of the plan."[11] I couldn't agree more.

You and I will never know the life that Christ died for us to live until we receive his great gift of grace. If you have never accepted your role as a member of his forever family, I ask you to do it now. Tell him that you need him and that you are ready for his leadership now. Turn away from your sinfulness, and position yourself for redemption instead. He longs to make his home in you, to direct you every step of the way.

If you are already a follower of Christ's, then remember the redemption that is yours! Repent of the things that are tripping you up, and claim ultimate freedom today. Whatever grief has been holding you bondage God can turn around into something good — but only when you fully surrender yourself to the Redeemer who makes *all* things new.

CHAPTER 9

Keeping the
Lampstand Lit

Joy runs deeper than despair.
—*Corrie ten Boom*

ON EASTER SUNDAY THIS YEAR, A MILITARY COUPLE WHO HAD BEEN married for twenty years and recently had relocated to Colorado Springs awakened to an unusual announcement from their three teenage sons. "It's Easter," one of them said on behalf of his brothers. "And we think our family should go to church." (Imagine if every teenager shared that sentiment!) The interesting thing was that this family had never been to church. *Ever.* Throughout twenty years of marriage and a decade and a half of raising kids, they'd never once set foot inside a church. But now the sons wanted to go. And it *was* Easter Sunday. Not wanting to say no to such a noble request, the parents went along with their boys' plan.

The family of five attended New Life's eleven o'clock service, where they heard a clear presentation of the gospel and realized for the first time that life could be far better than what they were experiencing. There could be unity in their marriage. There could be harmony in their home. There could be purpose to their days. There could be fulfillment in the deepest part of their souls.

Monday morning, following that churchgoing debut, the dad called New Life's offices and asked to speak to a pastor. An appointment was made, a meeting was set, and later that afternoon the man and his wife were sitting in the office of one of our pastors, explaining what a mess they had made of their marriage.

Sensing the couple's lack of knowledge about spiritual things, the pastor risked asking, "Do either of you know what it means to be born again?"

The man shook his head. "I've heard the phrase before," he said, "but I've never really understood what it meant."

The wife's blank expression was response enough.

Opening his Bible to John 3:1–6, the pastor forged ahead. "There is a story in the gospel of John about a high-powered guy who didn't really know what it meant either," he said. "Jesus had just explained to him that no one can see the kingdom of God unless he is born again, to which the man said, 'How can a man be born when he is old? Surely he cannot enter a second time into his mother's womb to be born!'

"Jesus then said, 'I tell you the truth, no one can enter the kingdom of God unless he is born of water and the Spirit. Flesh gives birth to flesh, but the Spirit gives birth to spirit.'"

The pastor looked up at the couple as he let his Bible fall shut, and noticed that they both had tears in their eyes. After letting a moment of silence hang in the air, he said, "Would you both like to be born again?"

By the time the man and his wife left New Life that day, they had been beautifully reborn. For the first time in their marriage, they felt a sense of joy well up, a sense that somehow, by God's newfound grace, they were going to be okay. And as the pastor relayed those events to me a few hours later, I was reminded of a fundamental truth that undergirds the Christian experience: joy always comes after redemption. It's never the other way around. The deep-seated satisfaction that couple had sought was never going to show up apart from God. Redemption must always precede joy.

Read how Psalm 30 bears this idea out:

> I will exalt you, O LORD,
>   for you lifted me out of the depths
>   and did not let my enemies gloat over me.
> O LORD my God, I called to you for help
>   and you healed me.
> O LORD, you brought me up from the grave;
>   you spared me from going down into the pit.
>
> Sing to the LORD, you saints of his;
>   praise his holy name.
> For his anger lasts only a moment,
>   but his favor lasts a lifetime;
> weeping may remain for a night,
>   but rejoicing comes in the morning.
>
> When I felt secure, I said,
>   "I will never be shaken."
> O LORD, when you favored me,
>   you made my mountain stand firm;
> but when you hid your face,
>   I was dismayed.
>
> To you, O LORD, I called;
>   to the Lord I cried for mercy:
> "What gain is there in my destruction,
>   in my going down into the pit?
> Will the dust praise you?
>   Will it proclaim your faithfulness?
> Hear, O LORD, and be merciful to me;
>   O LORD, be my help."
>
> You turned my wailing into dancing;
>   you removed my sackcloth and clothed me with joy,
> that my heart may sing to you and not be silent.
>   O LORD my God, I will give you thanks forever.

According to the psalmist David, he wasn't able to dance until *after* he'd been healed. He wasn't able to sing until *after* he'd been brought up from the grave. And he didn't experience being clothed with joy until *after* he'd been spared from the pit. Redemption precedes joy. It was true for the couple who surrendered their lives to Christ in my colleague's office. It was true for David, as he testified in the words of his psalm. And certainly it has been true for us as a church as we've sought to have our hope restored.

Days after that couple's conversion, I was spending some quiet time with God when I realized I was due to speak at the monthly all-staff meeting that was to be held the following morning. I love our staff meetings: we gather for breakfast, enjoy a time of worshiping God through song, and then explore the Scriptures together as one of the pastors on staff gives a brief talk. Typically, when I'm slated to speak, I simply share whatever is on my mind and heart. But this time I had no clue what to say.

After asking God for some guidance, I was prompted to read chapter 9 of the book of Esther. Initially I pushed back against this because nothing good happens in Esther chapter 9. "Are you sure you got the address right?" I silently asked God. By that point in the book, Queen Vashti has already been ousted, Esther has already been crowned the new queen, her cousin Mordecai has already been honored for uncovering the conspiracy to assassinate the king, the king's servant Haman has already plotted to extinguish all the Jews, Esther has already given her "if I perish, I perish" spiel, Mordecai has already gained power for exposing the plot to destroy his people, Haman has already been hanged on the gallows he had built for Mordecai, and the king has already issued his decree that would grant protection of all the Jews.

God seemed unfazed by my well-defended skepticism, so I turned to the book of Esther and headed straight for chapter 9.

I flew through the first nineteen verses and saw nothing of interest there. But then I hit verse 20 and realized that, of course, God knew what he was doing by sending me to this passage of Scripture on this particular day.

"Mordecai recorded these events," verses 20–22 report, "and he sent letters to all the Jews throughout the provinces of King Xerxes, near and far, to have them celebrate annually the fourteenth and fifteenth days of the month of Adar as the time when the Jews got relief from their enemies, and as the month when their sorrow was turned into joy and their mourning into a day of celebration. He wrote them to observe the days as days of feasting and joy and giving presents of food to one another and gifts to the poor."

Later, in verse 28, I read that those two days were to be remembered and observed in every generation by every family, and in every province and in every city. The days of Purim, as they were called, were to be faithfully celebrated by the Jews and prized by all of their descendants. As I mulled over those verses, it was as if God said, *I want you to declare your own season of Purim, the time when you and those you lead officially recaptured your joy.*

The next morning, I stood before the hundred or so people gathered for our meeting and recounted what I had found in Esther 9. "We're entering a season of Purim, gang. Let's mark *today* as the return of our joy."

Immediately after that statement, it was as if we had stepped inside an oxygen bar. I never would have ventured into Esther 9 on my own, but God knew that as a team—and, later, as a church—we needed a clear line of demarcation that designated the day our joy returned. Sure, we would always have troubles and trials to face and overcome, but finally *hope* had emerged. Joy was making a comeback in our midst.

I told the staff about the military couple who had surrendered their lives to Christ a few days before, and in response the entire room burst into cheers and applause. On every side, waves of energy washed over our group, the kind of natural-born vitality that surfaces when you are doing exactly what you were put on this planet to do. We had been delivered out of darkness, and now God was doing miracles among us. How could it get better than that?

It was such a simple salvation story, of a man and his wife coming to faith, but somehow it reminded the rest of the staff and me that God had not left our side. He remained among us. He remained *committed* to us. And despite the fiery trials we had been through, he still intended to use us for good. We had made a declaration on the Wednesday night following the shooting that we would not be governed by fear; this pronouncement of New Life's Purim was proof that we were living that out.

Often on the heels of great tragedy, I have found, grieving people need permission to smile again, to laugh, to rejoice. For example, the young widow who has lost her husband needs someone to come along at some point and say, "Hey, it's okay for you to date again. It's okay for you to enjoy life once more. It's okay for you to feel *joy*."

In front of the entire staff that day, I said, "Listen, it has been two and a half years since the shooting, and three and a half years since Ted's departure. It's okay for us to find our joy again. It's okay for us to celebrate what God is up to around here."

The collective exhale was nearly palpable. Everyone seemed ready to move forward; they just needed permission before they could start.

Beginning that week, our staff carried the message of recaptured joy to the congregation at large. Through weekend-service prayers, small group meetings, and impromptu hallway conversations alike, we invited everyone who calls New Life home to intentionally move ahead.

Despite an overwhelming number of congregants who leaped at the chance to have their sorrow turned to dancing, certainly there were some who still were wrestling with varying levels of pain. For example, I talked to a young dad shortly after that staff meeting who was describing the challenge his family still endured, all those months after the shooting. As he explained, on the afternoon when Matthew Murray stepped onto our campus, he and his wife were getting ready to leave the building with their three young kids. As soon as they heard gunfire, they rushed for the nearest exit. In their haste to seek shelter from what they assumed was a spray of bullets at their back, they quickly climbed into the van of a man they didn't even know. The total stranger had seen them ducking for cover, threw open the passenger doors, and urged, "Get in! Quick! I'll take you to your car."

Moments later the family of five found themselves just feet from their vehicle, which they had parked on the other side of the church. But as the dad jumped out of the van and opened the rear door to help his wife and kids into his family's own car, he was paralyzed by a horrifying sight. Less than ten feet from where he and his family stood lay Rachel and Stephanie Works, motionless and covered in blood. It was too late to shield his kids from the gruesome scene; the looks on their faces betrayed that they had already seen too much.

Understandably, those three young kids are traumatized still today. Even after months of counseling and countless conversations about life and death, good and evil, they still wrestle with difficult memories of the situation they took in that day.

But from what I'm hearing, stories like that are the exception. By and large, the core of our church is now ready to embrace a new day and to fully recapture the joy we once knew. For me to explain exactly *how* that joy was discovered, though, I need to rewind to January of this year.

The first Sunday of 2010 was the day the cloud of depression that had nearly enveloped my life somehow miraculously lifted. I was seated next to Pam during New Life's eleven o'clock worship service, when suddenly and unexpectedly I felt the burden I'd been carrying fall away. "Something big is happening to me today," I whispered to her. She nodded knowingly in reply, although she didn't yet fully grasp what I meant.

I took the platform to deliver my sermon and felt more energetic and optimistic as I climbed those half-dozen steps than I had felt in months. My gait was different. My posture was different. The strength of my voice was different. The congregation even looked better. I had no idea what God was up to, but I knew something had changed.

Following the service, I was bombarded with comments from congregants and staff who wanted to know what was up. "What happened to you up there?" they said. "You're not the same guy today."

It was only by hindsight that I would understand what was unfolding in my heart and in the heart of our church at large.

Immediately following that weekend worship service, the other pastors and I called New Life to a time of intentional prayer. We launched ten prayer meetings that occurred during the first full week of the year—early-morning meetings and nighttime meetings every day for five days straight. Not surprisingly, most of those gatherings were packed full. New Lifers somehow understood that if we were ever going to make progress as a church again, that forward movement would begin in prayer. More than a quarter-century ago, the church was birthed out of a prayer center in Louisiana that engaged in prayer walks throughout various neighborhoods. Out of that ministry, the World Prayer Center was established on New Life's campus, which launched the first twenty-four-hour online global prayer chain so believers could pray for real-time needs.

When I first came to New Life, I immediately recognized three key pillars marking our church's ministry. Other churches do these things really well, so they weren't necessarily unique attributes; they simply were obvious callings or mandates on this local body of believers. They include worship, missions, and student ministry—but *prayer* is what undergirds them all. Constant prayer. Fervent prayer. Prayer that expects great things of God.

Revelation 2 and 3 comprise messages from Christ to the seven churches in what was then called Asia Minor. But while the content was clearly intended for local churches in the first century, it's obvious the messages pertain to modern-day followers of Christ as well. After the shooting, as I reflected on the dark and tumultuous days that we as a church had faced, I couldn't help but think about the message in Revelation 2 to the church at Ephesus. "You have persevered and have endured hardships for my name, and have not grown weary," verse 3 says. "Yet I hold this against you: You have forsaken your first love. Remember the height from which you have fallen! Repent and do the things you did at first. If you do not repent, I will come to you and remove your lampstand from its place" (Rev. 2:3–5).

I mentioned in chapter 8 that we as a church had done our part to repent and to remember the marvelous redemption that was ours because of Christ's work on the cross. But what did it look like for us to cling to our first love? That was the question I sought to answer as we tried to find our footing once more.

In the first-century world, a lampstand served two purposes: because it typically was placed on a window ledge or in a corner of the front room, not only was it a means of providing light for those gathered inside, but also it was a way for guests to find your home. It was a signpost of sorts, a distinguishing characteristic that would tell your visitors they had arrived.

In that succinct passage of Scripture, I felt affirmed and admonished simultaneously. On one hand, God offered an acknowledgment that our church had patiently suffered for him without quitting along the way. But no sooner had that encouragement come out of his mouth than he issued a warning to those in Ephesus and to us: essentially, "If you don't return to your first love, your witness in this world will be nil."

I happen to believe that the primary reason why New Life did *not* become a used-car lot after a scandal and a shooting is that we never forsook our first love, an unwavering commitment to prayer. It was the way that we began as a church, and it would pave the path to reclaiming our joy.

* * *

I mentioned that roughly eighteen months after the shooting, I endured a bout of depression that threatened to knock me out of ministry altogether. Well, over the years I have learned two key things about transparency and vulnerability regarding sharing these experiences with others: first, they can be either helpful or harmful to your congregation and to you alike, and a discerning leader has to know which; second, good leaders always settle their personal issues in private — with God and a select group of close confidants — before they reveal them in a public setting. Because of those two beliefs, I didn't confess my depressed state to my congregation until I had a clear path out of the darkness I had stumbled into. It made for a lonely several months in terms of how I related with many of New Life's members, but once I saw the plane lifting off the tarmac, I divulged that while I'd been somewhat grounded for a while, I was finally getting airborne once more.

Not surprisingly, I learned soon after that confession that scores of New Lifers knew exactly how I felt. They too had faced shades of darkness and sought brighter days ahead. As I engaged in conversation and times of prayer with various people from our congregation, I saw a few themes emerge that had kept us from knowing deep joy. Perhaps you've seen one or two of these joy robbers show up in your life as well. If so, please take heart: hope doesn't have to stay hidden for long.

JOY ROBBER 1: Errant Expectations

Healing from life's heartbreaking events always takes longer than I think, and if you're anything like me, you get impatient with the process along the way. When I came to Colorado in August of 2007, I had so many dreams for the church. And yet before even one of them had the chance to take flight, a gunman foiled those plans.

The unexpected delay in seeing my big ideas come to fruition at New Life definitely robbed me of my joy. I wanted the pain of the shooting to go away, not only so our congregation could be healthy again but also so I could make my mark. God would deal with me regarding that ill-placed motivation by asking me to trust *his* timing, not mine.

The Sunday after the shooting, I learned of one New Lifer—an elderly woman—who circled our campus in her car for forty-five minutes straight and yet still couldn't bring herself to park and come inside. She had seen too much the previous week and now was utterly paralyzed by fear.

Months later David Works—father of Rachel and Stephanie—told me that he was at work one day when a colleague happened to drop a ream of paper on the tile floor. The *whap* that resounded caused a flood of bad memories to rush to David's mind.

My office is positioned directly upstairs from a chapel frequently used for times of worship by various groups, and every once in a while a drumbeat causes me to freeze. The similarity of that sound to a hit of gunfire triggers tough memories in me, and I'm taken right back to December 9. I've also noticed that although I used to enjoy watching police dramas on TV every so often, I can't tolerate them anymore. If a character wields a gun or gets shot himself, I'm done. The visuals are too much for me to handle.

I bring all this up because flashbacks are a very real thing. And getting past them can take some time.

Colorado Springs has a large military population, and most weeks our local papers include at least one story about the effects of post-traumatic stress disorder on the military personnel coming back from war. The more I read, the more I believe that witnessing violent events opens a door to our souls that frankly is quite difficult to close. To have expected our community of faith to get over the shooting quickly was a sure way to rob us of joy. Instead, we had to leave room for healing even as we pursued the joy that was ours to reclaim. We had to allow folks to heal at their own pace.

JOY ROBBER 2: Isolation and Insulation

Another joy robber we noticed along the way was the tendency for people walking through grief to isolate themselves from others and insulate themselves from the world at large. I was nearly guilty of it myself.

On the day of the shooting, my three closest friends were nowhere to be found. Pam was at home with our kids, Jeff Drott was watching over my family until I could get there, and Garvin McCarrell, who had moved from Dallas to serve on staff with me at New Life, had somehow gotten sequestered at the World Prayer Center and wouldn't be released until well after the police declared the crime scene safe. It was a strange feeling, walking through the most intense crisis of my life with people I barely knew. Jack Hayford provided incredible comfort, but how I craved the companionship of those I knew best.

Interestingly, I found that even after I was reunited with those three friends over the course of the coming weeks and months, I'd have to open myself up to the prospect of forging community where I didn't perceive that any existed. I needed to expand my heart to include on a deep level a select group of people at New Life whom I was just starting to get to know. And I had to trust them to flank me during a difficult time — something that is tough for any somewhat self-reliant person to do.

In her book *When I Lay My Isaac Down*, author Carol Kent recounts the harrowing tale of watching her highly decorated U.S. Naval Academy graduate son, Jason Kent, face a future of incarceration after shooting and killing his wife's ex-husband. Jason believed he was saving his two young stepdaughters from being abused by their dad, but of course the end didn't justify the means.

Several months into her agonizing journey, Carol and her husband received a note from a close friend who explained that God had prompted her to organize a loose network of loved ones, people who would supply emotional, physical, and monetary support as the Kents endured the unexpected valley they now faced. The friend called the group the Stretcher Bearers,[12] a name based on the biblical account found in Luke 5. In *The Message* paraphrase, verses 17–26 read as follows:

> One day as [Jesus] was teaching, Pharisees and religion teachers were sitting around. They had come from nearly every village in Galilee and Judea, even as far away as Jerusalem, to be there. The healing power of God was on him.
>
> Some men arrived carrying a paraplegic on a stretcher. They were looking for a way to get into the house and set him before Jesus. When they couldn't find a way in because of the crowd, they went up on the roof, removed some tiles, and let him down in the middle of everyone, right in front of Jesus. Impressed by their bold belief, he said, "Friend, I forgive your sins."
>
> That set the religion scholars and Pharisees buzzing. "Who does he think he is? That's blasphemous talk! God and only God can forgive sins."
>
> Jesus knew exactly what they were thinking and said, "Why all this gossipy whispering? Which is simpler: to say 'I forgive your sins,' or to say 'Get up and start walking'? Well, just so it's clear that I'm the Son of Man and authorized to do either, or both...." He now spoke directly to the paraplegic: "Get up. Take your bedroll and go home." Without a moment's hesitation, he did it — got up, took his blanket, and left for home, giving glory to God all the way. The people rubbed their eyes, incredulous — and then also gave glory to God. Awestruck, they said, "We've never seen anything like that!"

Similar to the people described in the gospel passage, the Kents' friends were simply people who recognized the family's needs and decided to take action. Or *not* to take action, which is sometimes the more powerful act of service. They sat with them. They listened without judging. They cared with selfless hearts. They came alongside the grieving family and bolstered their faith whenever it flagged.

As a pastor — the guy who typically is charged with exhibiting kindness and compassion toward people — I found it challenging initially to be on the receiving end of others' care. I felt guilty for having my own feelings of loss and compelled to turn my attentions toward those who "really" needed help. Fortunately, God would show me that by inviting others into my circumstances, I'd save myself boatloads of pain. By refusing to isolate and insulate over the long haul, I'd be a *far* healthier leader in the end.

When I was in the throes of depression, I received a phone call from my friend Robert Morris. The conversation wasn't all that memorable, but as we were getting off the phone, offhandedly I said something to the effect of, "You know, there are just some days when the weight of all this feels like way too much." The clock on my desk told me I was going to be late for my next meeting, so without giving Robert a chance to reply to my remark, I quickly said, "Gotta go. Love you, my friend. Will talk to you later. Bye." And with that, we hung up.

A couple days later Robert phoned me again. "Brady," he said, "we ended our last call kind of abruptly, and ever since then I haven't been able to shake something that you said."

Before I could brush aside his concern, he continued. "Are you thinking you can't keep doing this?"

We both knew the "this" he was referring to: *this* ministry role, *this* New Life thing, *this* post-scandal, post-shooting reality.

"I certainly have days when I wonder," I admitted.

Robert said, "Well, I want to be able to call and check on you more often, then. Can I do that?"

For more than a year, Robert called often, just to be sure I wasn't hanging out on any vocational cliffs. Those conversations were worth their minutes in gold.

Jimmy Evans is another example of a real stretcher bearer who showed up in my life. Jimmy is the kind of email communicator who can get *anything* said in two lines of text. I think I got three sentences one time and was tempted to print and frame the note. Well, one morning I received an email from him that filled my computer screen. I knew something big was up.

"Hey," the message began. "I woke up this morning with you on my mind. I feel strongly in my spirit that you have made the statement to yourself and perhaps are even believing in your heart that it would have been easier to go plant a church in north Dallas than to come lead at New Life Church. Is this true? Are you believing that message today?"

I had in fact confided in Pam — but *only* in Pam — that I wondered if a church plant would have spared us the immense pain we now were shouldering. I had no clue where Jimmy got his hunch.

Jimmy's email continued, "If this is true, then what you're thinking is all wrong. Planting a church would have been *very* tough. You would have done it, and you would have been successful to some degree. But you would have faced your share of giants there too. You need to settle in your mind that no matter what you would have said yes to, you would have had to slay some giants either way."

Jimmy's reminder proved incredibly useful to me; what he didn't know was that for weeks on end I'd been suffering from a grass-is-always-greener syndrome that was doing *nothing* productive for my soul. I had uprooted my entire family to relocate to Colorado Springs, and I wasn't satisfied. What was I supposed to do? Pam wondered what to do with that reality too. For a handful of months, she wrestled with how to support me when I was so clearly discouraged and distraught. To her credit, she refused to try to fix me and instead committed the concern to prayer. She gave me space without letting me isolate myself. She gave me solitude without letting me veer toward insulation. And she trusted our heavenly Father to call me back to the joy I had once known well. In short, she was the church to me, accepting and loving, present and available, willing to sacrifice for another's good. With few words but obvious actions, Pam perfectly modeled for me how to lead New Life to a far brighter day.

JOY ROBBER 3: Fatigue

There was a third joy robber that threatened to halt our church's progress, and that one was good old-fashioned fatigue.

In the life of any church, there are two times of the year when significant growth tends to occur. One is in September, at the start of the school and ministry year. The other is around the holidays, in December or early January. But for the first two years following the shooting, various problems had an uncanny way of cropping up during the very times when we were hoping to grow. I had thought that if I could just get the boat headed in the right direction, we'd find smoother waters somewhere along the way. But each time I'd think the wind was at our back, we'd slam headlong into a storm we hadn't seen coming. It was exhausting, to say the least.

In order for our joy not to be robbed altogether, I had to recognize that sometimes it pays bigger dividends to adopt a strategy of rest instead of trying to power your way through the pain. As a result, I sent all of the senior staff members on the staggered six-week sabbaticals I mentioned previously. I took some time off myself. I exhaled my frustration over the lack of productivity I saw at every turn and re-upped my commitment to letting God lead our church. In the end, we all benefited greatly from being well rested, well fueled, and strong.

In the past few months, I have counseled people in our church who were dealing with the loss of a business or a bank account, the agony of a spouse stuck in depression, the disillusionment of a prodigal teen, the despair over a bad medical report, and more. And to each of them I said, "Unless you find a way to get rest during this ordeal, the pain will do you in."

God never intended for us to shoulder our burdens in this life alone; instead, he wants us to let him help carry the load. And once our congregation caught sight of that truth, we saw hints of our joy come back.

JOY ROBBER 4: A Windshield That Has Become Dangerously Small

There is a reason why every car manufactured in this world has a small rearview mirror and a large windshield, which is that you and I are supposed to be far more focused on what is in front of us than on what we have just passed. But there were times after the shooting when New Life had things mixed up. We allowed our windshield to become tiny and our rearview mirror to captivate our every thought. And so one final joy robber I want to mention is this: the tendency to let your life's windshield become dangerously small.

Whenever we allow the backward-looking, past-oriented, rearview-mirror images to eclipse that magnificent work being accomplished before us and all around us, we miss real blessings that God is trying to pass our way. What's more, we give the enemy of our souls a foothold as he works to deflate our hearts.

Satan loves nothing more than when you and I fixate on our past. Don't give him that kind of satisfaction! Focus on the good you see happening, and on all that lies ahead. For us, one simple way this idea played out involved engaging in our Summer of Serving. Despite the two cataclysmic events we'd walked through, we called the church to rally together on behalf of our city, prayed fervent prayers asking for direction, and then worked to meet as many needs as we could possibly find. We planted gardens and repainted walls at the downtown rescue mission, we lifted the spirits of homebound elderly men and women who craved community, we cooked and delivered meals to families in need, and more. The acts of service didn't equate to quick progress in terms of our emotional healing, but they did help us shift our focal point from our own pain to the needs we could help meet.

And by taking that one small step of faith, our church was reaffirmed in our belief that God would use us in days to come to serve the poor, plant new churches, and catalyze transformed living in people whose paths we crossed.

At the heart of the original celebration of Purim, the Jewish people gathered together, remembered how God had provided them relief from their suffering, intentionally reclaimed their joy, and gave gifts to the poor. In the same way, we had so much to be thankful for; we just needed a forum for expressing it.

In addition to making the shift from wringing our hands in frustration and fear to using them to serve God and our community at large, we adjusted our posture in worship. For many months, during weekend services we had sung songs with titles such as "Overcome," "Never Be Shaken," and "Hiding Place." They are fantastic songs, but they are rearview-mirror songs. As we allowed God to enlarge our windshield, our worship leaders began writing anthems that helped our congregation move forward in powerful ways. "You Hold It All," "You Be the Change," and "Light Up the World" were all songs causing us to look forward. New Life's talented psalmists were singing us out of our pit. It's common for indigenous groups to leverage their art, their architecture, and their songs to reflect where they have been and where they're going, who they've been and who they are now. This has certainly been true for us as we've baby-stepped our way back to life.

Recently I came across an obscure passage in the book of Habakkuk that perfectly reflects the journey New Life took toward joy. Habakkuk 3:17 – 18 says, "Though the fig tree does not bud and there are no grapes on the vines, though the olive crop fails and the fields produce no food, though there are no sheep in the pen and no cattle in the stalls, yet I will rejoice in the LORD, I will be joyful in God my Savior."

In the same way that redemption must always precede joy, we learned the hard way that joy must always precede the promised harvest that is to come. Regardless of what calamity you and I face in this life, we must *choose joy* before new fruit can emerge. Remember, it is only *after* we set the oppressed free, share our food with the hungry, and provide the wanderer with shelter that our light breaks forth like the dawn and our healing quickly appears (Isa. 58:7–8).

During the three-week period immediately following our declaration of our own season of Purim, I had seven different families approach me following various weekend worship services and convey essentially the same story. "God told us to sell our house," they said, "gather up our belongings, and relocate to Colorado Springs so we could be part of New Life Church."

They came from Minnesota, Florida, Texas, north Denver—and not one of those families had any connection to our church. They just had the simple conviction that God would use them if they came. What they didn't know was that a close friend of mine had predicted their arrival. During a phone conversation we'd had a month or so before, he said, "Brady, for every leader you lose, a faithful leader will be given to you. For every servant you lose, a faithful servant will be provided. Trust God with the comings and goings during this season. He knows exactly what he is doing—and why."

It was a timely word that refreshed my heart. Plus, it has also proven true. God was preparing a vast harvest for us at New Life, if only we'd remember our redemption, reclaim our joy, and trust him with the sum of our days.

CHAPTER 10

Living by the Law
of the Farm

Thus says the LORD, "Just as I brought all this
great disaster on this people, so I am going to bring
on them all the good that I am promising them."
— *Jeremiah 32:42 NASB*

LEVI PATRICK WASN'T YOUR AVERAGE NINETEEN-YEAR-OLD. HOMECOM-
ing king, starting football player, New Life's youth-group leader with
a magnetic personality—the kid had everything going for him, until
one day last spring when his life came to an abrupt halt after a tragic
car accident.

In March 2010, Levi and three buddies were headed home from a
spring-break trip in Colorado, making their way across Interstate 70
in a Jeep Wrangler, when one of the back tires failed. The Jeep hit a
fence and rolled several times before three of the four young men were
thrown from the vehicle. The driver and two other passengers would
fare fine; Levi Patrick was pronounced dead at the scene.

One week prior to that fatal accident, Levi had gathered a group of
youth leaders from our church and said, "I want God to do something
huge at my school. I want my friends to wake up and realize that nothing else matters but Christ." Levi had been bold in sharing his faith

with his classmates and insisted on planting good seed. But he was hungry for impact. He wanted a *harvest*.

Now his parents were sitting in my office, asking the questions that every family who loses a loved one asks: Who are we now? What do we do now? Where do we go from here, now that this critical part of our family is gone?

New Lifers had asked the question twice in thirteen months: Who are we, now that Pastor Ted is gone? Who are we, now that the Works girls—not to mention our innocence—are gone?

Who are we now?

What do we do now?

Where do we go from here?

What do we do with this brokenness, God?

How are we supposed to go on?

Levi's parents scanned my face for answers, and I remember thinking, "You're not going to believe what I'm about to tell you, but I promise you it is true."

It had been more than two and a half years since the shooting, and I had seen God work miracles in our midst. "You won't always feel the way you are feeling today," I said to the Patricks. "I encourage you to take your time working through your understandable grief. But please remember that this valley won't last forever. There is a mountaintop on the other side."

I knew they didn't have ears to hear the fullness of what I was telling them. But I spoke the words anyway, knowing that one day in the not-too-distant future, those grieving parents would awaken to find their pain replaced with a promise—that each valley *always* comes to an end.

Rewind one week's time, to the day of Levi's memorial service held in the Living Room at New Life Church. I was seated near Levi's parents and noticed that as the service was about to begin, scores of people were still streaming into the auditorium, adding to the thousand or so who had already found seats.

One of our pastors eventually took the stage, and after acknowledging the marvelous impact of Levi's brief life, he gave a very simple presentation of the gospel. He explained that just seven days prior, Levi had prayed that a radical awakening for the things of God would occur in his high school and that his fellow students would be pointed to Christ.

Although it was a bit uncustomary for a funeral, the pastor then issued an altar call. How could he not? Hundreds of students from Levi's school were seated before him, and given Levi's final wish for his classmates to find Christ, the pastor felt it critical to give those kids a chance to respond to God's powerful offer of grace.

It is no exaggeration when I say that as the downbeat of the closing song reverberated throughout the room, hundreds of students flooded the stage. The five-foot-wide aisle between the front of the stage and the first row of seating was jam-packed with teary-eyed kids joyfully surrendering their lives to Christ. They had seen a real-deal Christian live out his faith and now grasped in fresh ways the fleeting nature of life. They had heard that more was in store for them, if only they'd let God lead their lives instead of frittering away their time.

As pastors and leaders huddled around each of those kids to pray with them and further explain the bold decision they were making that day, I thought about the profound impact even one devoted follower of Christ can have in this life. The following week in my office, during that meeting I had with Levi's grieving parents, Levi's mom looked me squarely in the eyes and said, "Levi would have gladly made this trade. He would have forsaken what remained of his earthly life just to give these kids a chance to know Christ."

I've thought about her comment dozens of times since that meeting, generally in the form of a question: If I knew that my suffering would somehow yield great kingdom fruit, would it change the way I walked through the inevitable pain this life brings? If you knew that *your* suffering might point people to Christ, would it alter your view of the valleys you'll face?

True, you and I are not meant to seek out suffering. God isn't looking for monks of old, known to inflict pain on themselves. But I'm coming to understand more and more that when suffering finds us — as it so often does — we can either view it as unwelcome, unfair, and destructive to our lives or see it as a worthwhile, necessary, and in some cases fruit-bearing path to purity.

It has struck me in the weeks and months since Levi's death that while many people may see only the potential that was lost on that day, perhaps God saw only potential *fulfilled*. One life well lived led to hundreds of people coming to Christ; as far as kingdom math is concerned, that is a sound return on investment.

If you have ever stuck a seed in the ground and later marveled when a plant popped up, then you understand the idea of potential. On this subject, Jesus says these words in John 12:24 – 26 (MSG):

> Listen carefully: Unless a grain of wheat is buried in the ground, dead to the world, it is never any more than a grain of wheat. But if it is buried, it sprouts and reproduces itself many times over. In the same way, anyone who holds on to life just as it is destroys that life. But if you let it go, reckless in your love, you'll have it forever, real and eternal.
>
> If any of you wants to serve me, then follow me. Then you'll be where I am, ready to serve at a moment's notice. The Father will honor and reward anyone who serves me.

Yes, Levi Patrick was just a nineteen-year-old kid when he died. He had his entire life ahead of him, decades and decades left to go. So much potential that would never be realized, so many memories that would never be made. This is how we view such a tragedy, isn't it? We see only the negatives, even as God suggests a different take.

Levi Patrick was one who let go of his life, reckless in his love for his classmates — for *everyone* he met. As a result, he drew in a harvest. He gained something far better than years on this earth. He gained a real and eternal life.

In the same way, when you and I are willing to let go of our lives, our ultimate potential gets immediately fulfilled. Our one single seed produces vastly more seed, which gives way to bushels of fruit.

When I was a kid, my dad frequently told me how much potential I had. "I love you, Brady," he'd say, "and I'm proud of the potential I see in you." But along the way, the sentiment became something of a burden to me. Was I living up to the potential he saw?

Later, after I had surrendered my life to Jesus Christ, I remember hearing that God saw potential in me too. And over the years, I have often wondered if I am living up to the possibilities he sees. I ask the question not to condemn myself but simply to evaluate my life. If it is true that before the beginning of time, God knew me and formed me and injected vast potential in my life (and it *is* true — read Psalm 139 for proof), then from time to time it's useful to sort out whether I'm doing what he intended for me to do.

And so I periodically perform a little self-examination: Am I giving my all for God's glory? Am I using the gifts and talents he has given me? Am I being a good steward of the resources I've been given? Am I applying the wisdom I've accumulated these past four-plus decades? How much of my life am I willing to surrender in order for my *fullest* potential to be known?

That last question is one that Jesus himself had to ask. Whenever I come across the story in Scripture of Jesus in the Garden of Geth-semane, I'm always drawn to the moment when he is about to be betrayed and must then journey toward crucifixion. Luke 22 says that after Jesus double-checked with his Father to be sure there really was no other way to redeem humankind than to die a gruesome death on a cross, an angel from heaven appeared to Christ and strengthened him. Knowing there was no other way, "and being in anguish, he prayed more earnestly, and his sweat was like drops of blood falling to the ground" (v. 44).

This was perhaps the most important prayer of Jesus' life. As blood perspired from his pores, Jesus had to decide how much of his life he was willing to give to God. Then and there, in the garden that day, Jesus had to determine whether he was a full-surrender sort of guy, a pivotal decision that makes the John 12 passage all the more significant.

Leading up to his grain-of-wheat spiel, Jesus told his disciples, in John 12:23, that the "hour has come for the Son of Man to be glorified." In other words, the hour had come for Jesus to lay down his life. "I tell you the truth," he said in verse 24, "unless a kernel of wheat falls to the ground and dies, it remains only a single seed. But if it dies, it produces many seeds." Then, in verses 27 and 28, Jesus said this: "Now my heart is troubled, and what shall I say? 'Father, save me from this hour'? No, it was for this very reason I came to this hour. Father, glorify your name!"

Here is how I read those verses, from Jesus' point of view: "Look, I know full well what tomorrow is going to hold if I agree to go through with this plan. I am going to endure pain on par with nothing else I have known. My reputation will be soiled. My spirit will be squelched. My body will be crushed. My life will be completely laid down. But what else am I to do? The whole reason for my existence is to glorify you, God. This is the very reason I came to earth. I knew this mission would require full surrender, and full surrender is what I will give. My life is in your hands, Father. Do with it what you will." He knew that his suffering would bear immense kingdom fruit, and that changed *everything* about how he endured the pain.

There is a critical lesson here for you and me both to learn. I don't believe that either of us will reach our full potential until we too arrive at that place where we are willing to lay it all down. I recognize that on all sides we are bombarded with a form of Christianity that seeks to make everything convenient, happy, and safe. But this is not the followership God called us to when he promised us persecution and pain. That life is mysterious. It is unpredictable. It is without boundaries. It is *decidedly* unsafe. But that fully surrendered life brings forth a harvest. It is that life that most glorifies God.

I want to walk you through what I have deemed the law of the farm, in order to give you a clearer picture of what this idea of full surrender truly means. See if this analogy from the natural world resonates with your experience.

Over the years, three passages of Scripture have informed my "law of the farm" theory. The first is one we just looked at, the verses in John 12. The second is 1 Corinthians 3:6–7, in which the apostle Paul says, "I planted the seed, Apollos watered it, but God made it grow. So neither he who plants nor he who waters is anything, but only God, who makes things grow."

In essence, God says, *If you want me to make something grow, then get busy planting some seed. Get busy watering it. Then I'll take responsibility for making it grow. I'll do my part as you do your part—that's the way this deal is going to work.*

The third Scripture that has influenced my thinking on this subject is 2 Corinthians 9:6. "Remember this," that verse says. "Whoever sows sparingly will also reap sparingly, and whoever sows generously will also reap generously." Give it *all* away, I understand those words to say, because whatever you give, you somehow get back. When we give mercy, we get mercy. When we give love, we get love. When we give grace, grace is what we receive in return. What a powerfully mind-boggling truth.

That brings us to the law of the farm, which I'll give to you in six simple steps.

Step one in the law of the farm is to *receive your God-given seed.* *Seed* in this sense includes things such as gifts, talents, abilities, money, time, and other resources. To live by the law of the farm—to live fully surrendered to God—we first must receive the seed he longs to give us, and do so with grateful hearts.

Step two is to *prepare the soil of your heart*. In Mark 4:1–20, Jesus tells the well-known parable of the sower. He describes four types of soil that a farmer's seed fell on: the path, the rocky places, the areas where thorns grew, and finally the good soil. But it was only when seed fell on good soil that a rich, exponentially productive crop was yielded.

So how do we turn our hearts into good soil? The answer is found by looking at the other three soil types: Jesus says that having a heart like the path is like learning his truth one day, only to allow Satan to snatch it from recollection the next. The Word of God was never fully anchored in the person, and as a result it was stolen away.

Having a heart like the rocky places means receiving God's truth with joy but then abandoning it as soon as challenging circumstances come along. That person never drew life from God's Word, and at some point he or she simply falls away.

Having a heart constricted by thorns means hearing God's truth in his Word but then allowing the worries of this life—the "deceitfulness of wealth and the desires for other things" (Mark 4:19)—to come in and choke the Word, making it unfruitful.

You and I must hold fast to the promises of God in order to live lives of complete surrender. Regardless of Satan's schemes, regardless of trying circumstances we can't predict, regardless of the shiny things vying for our attention, above all else we must cling to God's truth, knowing it is the *only* hope for our hearts.

Which brings us to step three: you've got to *plant your seed*.

As I mentioned, several years ago I faced a significant fork in my life's road. One path would lead me to plant a church in north Dallas or possibly take over a healthy church in one of two other states. The other would lead to New Life. When God whispered to me during that hotel-room conversation in Colorado Springs that perhaps the greatest use of my seed—the resources he has entrusted to me—was to help water a church that was desperately parched, I knew which path I had to take.

Part of the seed God gave me along the way was a promise that my life would be used for his glory if I would trust him by serving New Life Church. But it wasn't until I planted those seeds in faith—by uprooting my family from Texas, by relocating to Colorado, by jumping headlong into leadership in a brand-new church—that I was able to see God fulfill the promise he had made.

Clearly, there have been dark days along the way. But even when my role felt burdensome and my hope grew dim, I could look back in my mind's eye to that epic encounter with God, when he essentially said, *I'm calling you to this task, and I'll equip you to prevail. Just keep watering. Keep praying. Keep loving my people well.* This is what it means to plant our seed.

I read recently that a group of archaeologists uncovered a four-thousand-year-old Egyptian mummy in a tomb they had excavated, and as they carefully picked through the contents of that tomb, they located a small bag that contained remnants of wheat seed clutched in the mummy's hand. Tradition said the seed would serve as food for the deceased's journey into the afterlife, but what struck me about the story was one agronomist's assessment of that seed. He was quoted as saying that if just one of those seeds had been planted four thousand years ago and had been allowed to produce its full potential for even twenty years, at the culmination of that time period, it could have produced the annual wheat harvest for the entire world.

But the seed *didn't* produce a harvest like that; instead, it stayed clenched in the mummy's lifeless hand.

Untapped potential like that must frustrate our heavenly Father, especially in his kids, because if you have surrendered your life to Jesus Christ, then you are part of the harvest of Jesus' having said yes to pain and suffering, yes to being ridiculed, yes to dying on a cross. And the reason why he said yes to those things was so we could live in *abundance* instead of in the scarcity of sin. He died so we might live —really *live*. He paid the price so we could be let off the hook. And what he asks for in return is a life fully surrendered to him.

We are called to lay down the sum of our lives. We are called to *plant* our good seed.

One aspect of my role as pastor that grieves me most is meeting with a married couple on the verge of divorce. In almost every instance, by the time that twosome makes it to my office, they can't stand each other, and fighting has become their primary means of communication. They are literally days away from phoning the attorneys, but as a last-ditch effort, they come meet with me, a "please fix us" look on their faces.

Truth be told, I would love nothing *more* than to fix them. But they and I both know I can't. All I can do is declare the obvious: "You two are eating the harvest that is being yielded from whatever seed you planted years ago." Those are the exact words that come out of my mouth.

The fact is, nobody wakes up one day and says, "Gee, I think I'll get a divorce today." More likely, years ago one or both spouses planted seeds of criticism, apathy, or discontent in the marriage, and eventually those seeds bore fruit. That fruit typically involves frustration, resentment, and anger and often ultimately leads to divorce.

Whenever I meet with couples like that, I ask, "How long did it take you to get to my office?"

"Oh, just about fifteen minutes," they'll usually reply. "Traffic wasn't all that bad."

I stare at them until they catch my drift, and then the truth of the matter comes out.

"Five years," "Twelve years," "Twenty years," they'll report. Or longer in some cases.

"It took you all that time to get here," I'll say, "and in one hour of counseling, I'm supposed to right all your wrongs?"

What I wish I could tell those couples, long before they darken my doorstep, is to start planting good seed *today*. Instead of sowing criticism, sow a word of encouragement. Instead of sowing expectations, sow a selfless act of service. Instead of sowing discontent, sow a prayer of gratitude to God for something you actually *enjoy* about your mate. I guarantee that the trajectory of those marriages will shift, if only those couples would plant a little good seed. The challenges they face in their relationships may not disappear overnight, but the eyes of their hearts will be opened to seeing God's perspective on things.

The seed God places in your hand and mine is good seed that he promises will bear worthwhile fruit. But we'll never see tomorrow's harvest unless we're willing to scatter it today.

Step four in the law of the farm is to *water your seed*. Throughout Scripture, water is synonymous with the presence of God. For example, during his conversation with the Samaritan woman at the well, Jesus said that everyone who drinks water from a manmade well would be thirsty again, but "whoever drinks the water I give him will never thirst. Indeed, the water I give him will become in him a spring of water welling up to eternal life" (John 4:14).

In the same way that Jesus was willing to quench the eternal thirst of the Samaritan woman's soul, he wants to quench our souls' thirst as well. By his Spirit, he promises us his constant presence, if only we'll let him stay near. And it's only by inviting him near that a harvest can someday be produced.

Step five of living by the law of the farm is that you must *voluntarily pull some weeds*. Since the shooting, I have certainly pulled my share of weeds. In an effort to rid our community of deception and pain, I turned over as many rocks as I could find. And I discovered lots of bugs underneath. There were hurt feelings and unfortunate misunderstandings and people who made unnecessary departures from our church. Sure, we had experienced a terrific, quenching "rainfall," but you know as well as I do that rain can also produce weeds that, left to do as they please, can choke a healthy crop.

Pulling those weeds required more humility than I and others have ever had to manifest. It required prayer, perseverance, and dozens of sincere apologies on all of our parts. But in the end, it allowed space for a harvest that thankfully soon would appear.

Whenever I talk with folks about the law of the farm, I ask them to guess the sixth and final step, and 99 percent of the time they get it wrong. Step six, contrary to popular opinion, is simply to *wait*. After acquiring the seed, preparing the soil, planting the seed, watering the seed, and diligently pulling the weeds, the farmer's most critical remaining task is to have faith that the harvest will come.

In the Old Testament, Abraham had the seed of a promise from God, and a heart receptive to being used for good. He planted his seed, he watered his seed, and he was faithful to pull the weeds. But when it came time for that sixth and final step, he bailed on the process altogether and chose to go his own way in life. He refused to wait. Instead, he pushed aside God's faithful promise and bore his son Ishmael through a servant rather than trusting that God would accomplish those plans through his wife.

Then there was Joseph, another Old Testament hero of the faith, who had to go through the pit, the prison, and the palace before he'd see God fulfill the promises he had made. Unlike Abraham, though, after he had done all he could do, Joseph willingly agreed to just wait.

As I write this chapter, it is springtime in Colorado. We've endured a long and somewhat hard winter for this part of the country, and I am more than ready for the seasons to change. In front of my house are a dozen or so perennial bushes that have been lying dormant all winter. Before temperatures began to plummet, I cut them back and covered them in mulch to protect them from the multiple snowstorms I figured they would have to endure, and throughout those bone-chilling months, I'd frequently look out the front windows, find three or four feet of snow blanketing my bushes, and wonder whether the flowers would ever come back.

Just this morning, as I made my way to the office, I noticed that a few green sprouts had shown up. The seeds had been properly planted, watered, and kept weed-free, and yet *still* it surprised me to see a small harvest begin to appear—which tells you something about my faith from time to time. After all, if I struggle to believe that a silly daylily bulb will keep its promise, imagine what I do with the assurances of God.

God's Word says that we *will* reap what we sow. It says that if we sow things such as joy, hope, and expectancy, our tomorrows will be brighter than today. When we sow the good seeds he places in our hands, our future will be *full* of good things. And yet if you're anything like me, you have your moments when these truths are difficult to accept.

Still, even if we went into the process kicking and screaming, those of us who call New Life home learned to wait on God when our desired timing didn't line up with his. We wanted the microwave version of healing, but God had something entirely different in mind. In hindsight, I am so glad we submitted to his plans, now that I see the harvest he had in store for us all along.

Sometimes the crop begins to bud without fanfare, and sometimes the experience winds up being a bit more dramatic. Case in point: Several months ago a devoted young man from our congregation named Michael was deployed from Fort Carson, an army base in Colorado Springs, to Afghanistan. Soon after arriving, Michael was introduced to a member of his brigade named Miles, a self-proclaimed adherent to witchcraft.

Over time, the two developed a close friendship. Instead of judging him, condemning him, preaching at him, or spending every waking hour trying to convert him to Christianity, Michael simply loved Miles well and stayed focused on being his friend. Eventually the witch began asking his newfound buddy questions about Jesus and about Christianity. Michael answered the questions as clearly and plainly as he could, being careful not to force his view on Miles.

One day, while both men were out on a mission, Michael got caught in a firefight and took a bullet to the chest. Miles later would say of the experience, "Most men are panicky and fearful when they are about to die, but not Michael. I had never before seen peace on a person's face during the last, painful moments of life, but that's exactly what I saw come over him as he faded away."

In that moment, Miles wondered if faith in Jesus Christ just might be worth checking out.

Fast-forward to several weeks later, when Miles was back in Colorado Springs after completing his tour of duty. Following our final Sunday morning service, I was greeting a long line of people who had stopped by to meet some of our pastoral staff and gather more information about our church, and out of the corner of my eye I caught sight of a guy standing against the far wall. He wasn't in line, but he was obviously waiting on me. Something about him seemed a little off. His brow was furrowed, his shoulders were slumped, and he projected a disgruntled vibe. I noticed that as I engaged in conversation with each person in line, the man's eyes stayed trained on me. I definitely wanted to know what was on his mind.

Eventually there was a small opening in the line, and I glanced at the man as if to grant him permission to cut. Immediately he carved his way toward me, introduced himself — his name was Miles — and explained that he had been a practicing witch his entire life but that he'd had a life-changing experience in Afghanistan. "I remember a buddy of mine named Michael talking about this church on several occasions, about how everyone is welcomed here. I've sat in the back of your auditorium these past three Sundays and have listened to every word you've said. I guess I've never really heard the gospel explained like that, and I wonder what I need to do next."

I applauded the man's courage for being willing to talk to someone about the questions God was laying on his heart, and then I introduced him to my friend Garvin, who was already standing at my side.

"Miles, you can trust this man," I said as I nodded toward Garvin. "He'd love to talk with you for a few minutes and help you get a few things sorted out."

As a result of the one-on-one conversation that ensued, Miles surrendered his life to Jesus Christ and said he was ready to be baptized. Just one thing stood in his way: our monthly baptism service wasn't taking place for three more weeks, and Miles was about to be deployed for his second trip to the Middle East. He asked what could be done.

One week later thirty born-again soldiers who attend New Life convened one morning inside our building known as the Tent and cheered and applauded and cried as they witnessed Miles declaring publicly his faith in Christ. At this writing, Miles is back in Afghanistan serving our country, but also serving our God. One man's life, radically changed—pure evidence of harvesttime.

Almost exactly one year prior to Miles's conversion experience, I was standing at the front of the auditorium following a worship service, when a man wearing a floor-length trench coat and black military boots stormed toward me, reached inside his jacket, and eyed me with obvious disdain. It all happened so quickly that I didn't have time to react. The sole thought that floated through my mind was, "I'm going to be killed, right here, right now."

From inside his jacket, he pulled out a large pentagram necklace dangling from his neck. In one quick movement, he ripped the chain off, threw the Wiccan symbol to the floor, and said, "I can't wear this anymore." I'm sure my eyes were the size of half-dollars as I took in his lightning-fast move. "I want to be born again," he said with strength in his voice. "And I want it to happen today."

As it turned out, the guy had headed up a witchcraft group in a neighboring community for more than two decades. One week after his conversion, he and his wife showed up on our campus with a van full of satanic paraphernalia and asked if our pastors would help them burn it all.

On an otherwise-ordinary Tuesday morning, several of our pastors lit a fire in a fifty-five-gallon drum in our north parking lot and loaded it with everything from horned goats' heads that had been used in various blood rituals to books on sorcery. The couple renounced their former beliefs, they agreed to be water baptized, and they asked us to rededicate their children, this time to the Lord Jesus Christ. I see them around New Life frequently these days and still shake my head in wonder over the transformation they've undergone.

Having even a small role in seeing lives radically transformed — it's what New Lifers love most about being the church of Christ.

I said those very words recently to a group of ministry leaders who had flown all the way to Colorado Springs to attend and evaluate our Friday night gathering of more than one thousand college students and twentysomethings who collectively call themselves the Mill. The leaders wanted to know how we were attracting so many kids, and as we toured the room where the Mill meets every week, I could tell that their questions only multiplied. The program is run on a shoestring budget. The stage is dilapidated and desperately needs to be replaced. The projection screens are old. The technology is dated. The couches are mostly threadbare. And yet each and every Friday night, the place is packed with worship-crazed kids.

I knew exactly what the church leaders were thinking, even before they uttered a word. "Where is all the … *stuff?*" they wondered. They wanted to know where we were hiding our hoopla — the stimulating stage decor, the fancy lighting, the interesting seating, the secrets to our undeniable success.

Eyeing the men and women who had come all this way to be sorely disappointed, I said with a smile, "What you see is what you get."

"But wait," one of them braved. "If this is all there is, then why are all these kids coming here week after week?"

Right about then, the opening song set started, and I pointed our group to our seats. The Mill's pastor, Aaron Stern, took the stage and said plainly, "Welcome to the Mill, everyone. We're here to worship God, to read the Scriptures, to pray, and to live life unified. Let's get going."

And that was that. Nothing fancy. Nothing flashy. Nothing over the top. Just a bunch of kids seeking Christ with full hearts of faith, mixed with the power and presence of God. Harvesttime, pure and simple. When you and I commit ourselves to full surrender, the harvest *never* fails to appear.

In two months' time I will celebrate my third anniversary as senior pastor of New Life Church. And among the promises of God I'll be clinging to is the one that says he will be faithful to repay his children for the time the locusts ate. The metaphor is from Joel 2:25 and comes after God's promise to deliver a harvest of new grain, new wine, and new oil to his people. It's as though God says, *I know I've allowed you to endure some seriously tough times, but if you'll hang in there, you'll see that I'm about to make all things good.* It's a sentiment I take to heart, because it's exactly what he is doing in our midst.

What is happening at New Life Church is nothing short of a miracle. Most churches splinter into half a dozen disparate groups on the heels of severe suffering such as what we at New Life experienced. And yet this body is beautifully defying the odds by growing, thriving, having *impact* in our world. Churches are being planted. People are getting saved and baptized. Followers of Christ are living righteous lives. It's what the harvest looks like when we fully surrender to God.

In the past six months alone, we have sent hundreds of people on mission trips, investing both money and followers of Christ in more than thirty nations around the world. We have blessed our city with truckloads of household items and clothing and stocked local food banks with ongoing food-drive efforts. Plans are in the works to launch several Dream Centers in our area to come alongside people in dire straits and help them back on their feet, which represents the fulfillment of a year-long dream. For several months in 2010, several New Life pastors and I met with city, military, and other ministry leaders and discovered there were significant people groups in our city who are underserved. Which is where the Dream Center concept comes in. These safe havens will allow the people of New Life Church to be mobilized in caring for our city by meeting those unmet needs. If all goes according to plan, our first Dream Center will be a medical clinic for women and will open in early 2011.

I wish I could attribute these successes to my smarts as a leader, but you'd see through the thin facade. The truth is that God has kept his hand on this group of believers and is committed to using us for his glory throughout the earth. He has protected us. He has blessed us. And he has promised to stay by our side. This is who we are now, after terrible loss: We were persecuted, but we are not in despair. We were struck down, but we are not destroyed. We have grieved, but not as those who have no hope. Today we're simply a collection of devoted Christ followers determined to serve our God.

My friend Jimmy Evans talked to a farmer in west Texas one year during an uncharacteristically warm winter and said, "You must be *loving* this mild weather!"

The farmer replied, "Nothing could be further from the truth. We need cold winters to keep our crops alive; that's what kills the bugs, keeps the springtime weeds from taking over the crops, and helps the soil thrive, come spring. Without a good, hard freeze, we'll have a horrible harvest next year."

Jimmy told me that story in passing, but it has stuck with me. Sometimes you and I need suffering—a good, hard freeze—in order to grow as God intends for us to grow. Suffering has a strange way of pruning us and preparing our hearts' soil to thrive. It may take three days, three years, three decades, or more for those tiny green shoots to show up, but a harvest *will* one day appear. We have to remember that winter won't last forever, even when all around us is frozen and bleak. Springtime is always just one season away, those days of newness and refreshment, redemption and healing, laughter and beauty and joy.

"Thank You, Thank You, Thank You ..."

Because he is God,
from whom all blessings flow,
thankfulness is the best way
to draw near him.
— *Sarah Young*

THREE DAYS AFTER THE SHOOTING AT NEW LIFE, OUR CONGREGATION and thousands from the Colorado Springs community gathered in our auditorium to grieve together, to worship God together, and to publicly declare that fear would not govern our lives. At the end of that two-hour worship service, my friend and mentor Pastor Robert Morris took the platform to offer a closing prayer. I'll never forget how he began: "Thank you, thank you, thank you," he said to God. "Thank you, thank you, thank you that every plan of the enemy has always backfired, that this plan too will backfire, and that the witness and influence and anointing on New Life Church will increase by the Spirit of God."

Pastor Robert went on to thank God for still being on his throne even when tragedy unfolds in our lives. He thanked him that the crown had not fallen from his head. He thanked him that somehow, some way, people would actually come to faith in Christ because of the awful events of December 9. He thanked him that even in a trial, God is there.

I remember being incredibly moved by my friend's prayer, even as I questioned whether I was really ready to thank God for all that had just happened. Spiritually, I knew that gratitude — even for life's toughest circumstances — was the right response. But practically, I wasn't quite there. Devastation, disillusionment, staring evil directly in the face — I'd uprooted my family from our comfortable life in Texas for *this*?

Obviously, it was going to take some time for the words *thank you* to form on my lips.

I learned something years ago that came to mind recently. It relates to *dendrochronology*, which is just a big word for analyzing a tree's life based on the rings on its trunk that have formed throughout the years. It came to mind because I was roaming through a dense part of the forest near my home and ran across a series of trees that had been felled by lightning. I stared at the cross section of one of those trees and noticed an irregular pattern of thick and thin rings moving out from the trunk's center in concentric circles.

I'm not adept at reading tree rings, but according to fifteen minutes of a show I caught on the Discovery Channel one time, people who *are* good at reading them can tell you with amazing accuracy how many forest fires, droughts, and beetle infestations a particular tree has withstood in its lifetime, as well as how many healthy years it has known, all by scrutinizing those rings. Which made me wonder what New Life would look like, if you cut our church in half and looked inside. I have a feeling you'd find lots of thick rings in the center, representing years and years of great growth, followed by narrow rings representing scandal and the loss of two innocent young girls. But what energizes me is the idea that just outside of that narrowing, I believe you'd find increasingly wider rings once more — signs of redemption, renewal, and restoration.

As I looked more closely at one of the trees at my feet, I saw a cluster of tiny green roots bursting forth on the very branch that had once been declared dead. The tall spruce had fallen, but it was claiming new life as its own. The significance of that unforeseen recovery wasn't lost on me, for I am experiencing something similar these days.

In the quiet of the forest, I was reminded that all of us — both those who call New Life home and every Christ follower alive today — are surrounded by a cloud of witnesses, as Hebrews 12 calls them, women and men who valiantly suffered for their faith. These are the ones who stared down Satan and remained unshaken. They planted the early churches, prayed fervent prayers, and laid the firm foundation on which we now stand. They're the martyrs we sing about in worship songs, the ones who died for the sake of God's glory and did so with the joy of the Lord on their faces, the ones who will cheer us across the heavenly finish line someday. As I considered afresh the sacrifices they'd made, I couldn't help but wonder what they see when they look down from their celestial seats and peek into Christ followers' lives today. Do they see a bunch of beaten-down believers limping their way through life, or do they see the strength of Christ made manifest as his followers claim his promises as their own?

Staring at those hope-filled green roots, I thought to myself, "I refuse to limp into heaven someday. If my two choices are becoming a victim or becoming a victor, a victor is what I will be." Admittedly, on more occasions than I care to admit over the past three years, I have whined to God, "I did *not* sign up for this!" But each time, somehow with lovingkindness to spare, I sensed God say in reply, *Zip it, Brady.* I took that to be shorthand for this train of thought: *Remember who you are. Remember whose you are. Remember the seal of my Spirit that has been graciously placed on your life. Remember the power that is now yours because of my unwavering presence in your life. Stand up. Dust yourself off. Commit yourself to the path of progress once more. There is a mountaintop on the other side. And the view is far better from there.*

The apostle Paul offered a similar set of reminders to the church at Ephesus, a group of people who were living under Roman bondage and the oppression of the occult somewhere in Asia, knowing that the outlook for their survival was pretty bleak. One day, probably while they were camped out in a bare cave adjacent to the Mediterranean Sea, some of those Ephesians received a letter from their leader, a guy who himself was in a Roman prison. Can you imagine their delight?

The first part of that letter begins as follows:

> Ever since I heard about your faith in the Lord Jesus and your love for all the saints, I have not stopped giving thanks for you, remembering you in my prayers. I keep asking that the God of our Lord Jesus Christ, the glorious Father, may give you the Spirit of wisdom and revelation, so that you may know him better. I pray also that the eyes of your heart may be enlightened in order that you may know the *hope* to which he has called you, the riches of his glorious inheritance in the saints, and his incomparably great power for us who believe. That power is like the working of his mighty strength, which he exerted in Christ when he raised him from the dead and seated him at his right hand in the heavenly realms, far above all rule and authority, power and dominion, and every title that can be given, not only in the present age but also in the one to come. And God placed all things under his feet and appointed him to be head over everything for the church, which is his body, the fullness of him who fills everything in every way.
>
> —*Ephesians 1:15–23, emphasis added*

It was a letter sealed with a promise, a promise of hope. A promise of power. A promise of *ultimate fulfillment*, courtesy of the God who fills everything in every way. How I need those things in my life too. Granted, I have no idea how everything is going to pan out for us at

New Life. We could face another monumental crisis tomorrow that will level us and leave me whining once more. But what is true today will still be true then: I can choose in that moment to believe God, or I can settle for living a victim's small life. I can limp my way through that valley, or I can leap toward the mountaintop. I hope I'll choose the victor's approach, the path that is paved with hope. And regardless of how challenging are the circumstances I face, I pray that a sincere *thank you* is found on my lips.

Bible Versions

The following Bible versions are used in this book in addition to the New International Version (NIV):

Notes

1. Jonathan Acuff, *Stuff Christians Like* (Grand Rapids: Zondervan, 2010), 115–16.

2. Name changed to protect identity.

3. N. T. Wright, *After You Believe: Why Christian Character Matters* (New York: HarperOne, 2010), 103.

4. Ibid., 104.

5. Randy Alcorn, *If God Is Good: Faith in the Midst of Suffering and Evil* (Colorado Springs: Multnomah, 2009), 12–13.

6. www.thebiblechannel.org/Missions_Quotes/missions_quotes.html.

7. www.youtube.com/watch?v=GlZtEjtlirc.

8. Helen H. Lemmel, "Turn Your Eyes upon Jesus" (1922, public domain).

9. G. K. Chesterton, *Orthodoxy: The Romance of Faith* (San Francisco: Ignatius Press, 1908).

10. Elisabeth Kübler-Ross, *On Death and Dying* (New York: Scribner, 1997).

11. John MacArthur, *The Promise of Redemption*, part 1, tape GC 90–247, *www.gty.org*.

12. The Kents' friend gives credit for the term to Pastor Michael Slater, author of the book *Becoming a Stretcher Bearer* (Ventura, Calif.: Regal, 1985), formerly published under the title *Stretcher Bearers* (Stretcher Bearer Ministries, PO Box 1035, La Habra, CA 90633-1035).

Share Your Thoughts

With the Author: Your comments will be forwarded to the author when you send them to *zauthor@zondervan.com*.

With Zondervan: Submit your review of this book by writing to *zreview@zondervan.com*.

Free Online Resources at
www.zondervan.com

Zondervan AuthorTracker: Be notified whenever your favorite authors publish new books, go on tour, or post an update about what's happening in their lives at www.zondervan.com/authortracker.

Daily Bible Verses and Devotions: Enrich your life with daily Bible verses or devotions that help you start every morning focused on God. Visit www.zondervan.com/newsletters.

Free Email Publications: Sign up for newsletters on Christian living, academic resources, church ministry, fiction, children's resources, and more. Visit www.zondervan.com/newsletters.

Zondervan Bible Search: Find and compare Bible passages in a variety of translations at www.zondervanbiblesearch.com.

Other Benefits: Register yourself to receive online benefits like coupons and special offers, or to participate in research.

ZONDERVAN®

ZONDERVAN.com/
AUTHORTRACKER
follow your favorite authors